The BAROMETER

Your home weather forecaster

by

Ron Lobeck

(TV Weatherman)

Illustrations and photographs by the Author
(with exceptions)

This one is for the "girls" in my life.

Pamela, Kath, Kim, Katie, Sarah and Faye . .

ISBN 1 873953 01 1

Introduction

The Barometer . . . A lot of people have one, probably it was obtained as a Christmas present from the nearest and dearest, or maybe as a retirement gift from former work colleagues. There it hangs on the wall, in the hall . . . Perhaps it is one of the lucky ones, because it gets the occasional tap with the forefinger, and its dial is scrutinised. The weather words indicated by its pointer are noted and taken as 'the forecast'. It is always correct, (unlike that chap on the telly). Good old barometer . . . !

On the other hand it may be one of those that is viewed with some suspicion, because 'it doesn't work'! The weather words never seem to match up with what is happening outside. It points to 'Fair' and outside it is raining cats and dogs! There is obviously something wrong with it . . . and so it clings forlornly to the wallpaper, a part of the decorations. Wasted, because its true function is not understood.

Why is it that in one case the barometer is religiously believed and in the other it is an object of mistrust?

What is a barometer? Well one thing it is not: it is not the complete answer to the problems of weather forecasting. I wish that it was that simple! Another thing a barometer is not: it is not an ornament, although in many cases that is why it is bought, and what it tends to become, mainly because of the above mentioned lack of understanding.

The principle of the barometer has been described as the most important discovery in meteorology. Even though barometers can be designed and constructed in different ways, that fundamental principle always applies.

As we shall discover one type can be readily adapted for other purposes.

The barometer that is most commonly to be found today is nothing like the device first invented. However, no matter what the shape or design they all have one thing in common: they are in fact scientific instruments.

Used properly they can be useful tools for making predictions about 'the weather'.

Nevertheless, there are many factors that can interact to generate or change 'the weather' and in order to gain full value from the barometer it is necessary to look at some of the processes that take place in the atmosphere, which give rise to such changes or local variations.

Only with an understanding of the way in which a professional forecast is built up, can you hope to get better at making your own forecasts.

So that is the aim of this book: to give you an insight into what your barometer can do and show how the information it provides fits into the overall pattern in terms of making a weather forecast.

Hopefully, at the end you will not only be in a position to get much more enjoyment and useful information from what is one of the oldest and most reliable of meteorological instruments, but also, test your forecasting skills against those of the media specialists!

But how did it all begin . . . ?

CHAPTER ONE

'When two Englishmen meet, their first talk is of the weather . . .'

These words were spoken by Dr Samuel Johnson in the 18th century and are a true reflection of the worldwide recognition of the *British* fascination with the weather. In view of this fact it is somewhat surprising to find that the barometer was invented by an *Italian*.

Evangelista Torricelli was born in Faenza, Italy in 1608. He studied at the University of Rome and subsequently replaced the great astronomer Galileo as mathematician at the Florentine Academy.

Apart from his interest in the movements of the Earth, Moon and stars, Galileo also studied other phenomena and amongst his work were results that showed it was impossible to raise water more than about 10 metres (33ft) by means of a single stage suction pump.

This interested Torricelli who set out to develop something that:

'. . . might show the changes of the air, sometimes heavy and coarse, now light and more subtle . . .'

Which suggests that he was aware of atmospheric changes and perhaps their connection with 'weather'.

Following the suggestions of Galileo he took a narrow glass tube about 1m(3ft) in length which was sealed at one end. Next he completely filled the tube with mercury (quicksilver). Covering the open end of the tube with his finger he inverted it and placed it below the surface of a reservoir of mercury. Securing the tube in a vertical position he removed his finger to discover that rather than flowing out, the mercury in the tube fell to a certain level where it remained.

Mercury is a metal and is a liquid at normal temperatures and pressures . . .

Torricelli realised that something must be supporting the mercury column and this he correctly identified as the air pressure.

Further experiments proved that the space above the mercury was a vacuum and this became known as 'Torricelli's vacuum'.

The height of the mercury column was about 76cm(30in) but over a long period, study revealed that it was not constant. In fact it often varied, sometimes from day to day, and even over shorter periods.

Torricelli concluded that such variations were the result of changes in the atmospheric pressure, but he never published these findings. It was left to others to exploit this aspect of the instrument.

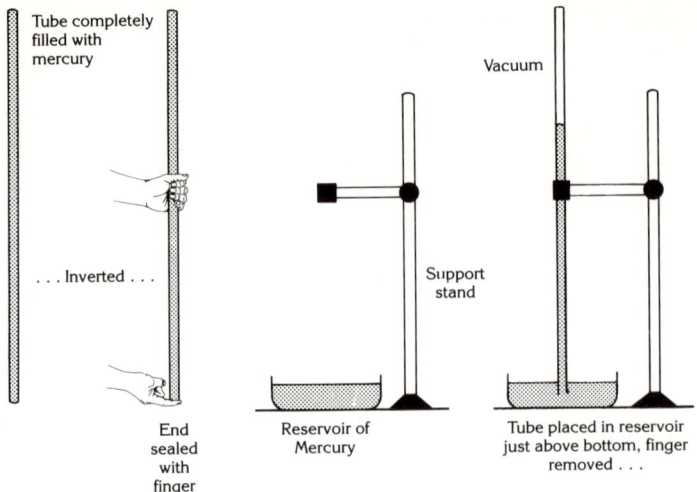

Torricelli's Experiment

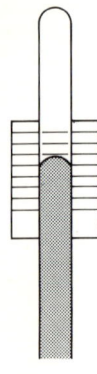

Mercury
Meniscus

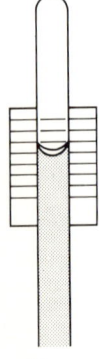

Water
Meniscus

Nevertheless, in 1643 the mercury barometer was effectively invented.

But what is the relationship between Galileo's discovery that water could not be lifted above about 10m(33ft) by a single stage suction pump and the height of the mercury column supported inside Torricelli's glass tube?

The answer lies in the difference in the densities of the two liquids. Mercury is very dense and is about 13.5 times denser than water.

Thus, if we divide 10m(33ft) by 13.5 the answer is 0.76m or 76cm(30in), which is the average height of the mercury column.

Another way of looking at it is to consider building a barometer using Torricelli's method, but filling the tube with water rather than mercury. Taking into account the normal range of air pressure we would require a tube at least 13m(43ft) in height.

Not a very practicable instrument!

Mercury has an extra advantage over water as a liquid suitable for use in a barometer apart from its high density it also has a meniscus that is curved in a way that makes it easy to read, unlike water which because of its high surface tension tends to stick to the inside of the tube.

"Just popping out to read the barometer, dear . . ."

But what is happening inside the glass tubes?

Whether they are filled with mercury or water the weight of the liquid in the column is exactly balanced by the weight of air pressing down on the surface of the excess liquid in the reservoir.

Thus, in this form the barometer can be thought of as a balance. This leads to the concept of Atmospheric pressure being the weight of air above a particular point on the Earth's surface.

Which explains the derivation of the name: barometer; it comes from the Greek 'baros' meaning 'weight'.

We do not talk of 'weight' but rather 'pressure' which in this case is 'weight per unit area'.

For every 10m(33ft) increase in depth in water the pressure increases by one atmosphere . . .

For a normal atmosphere the pressure at sea level is about 1 kilogram per square centimetre (14.7 pounds per square inch).

However, these are not the units you will be familiar with on your barometer scale, and we shall look at what they mean later.

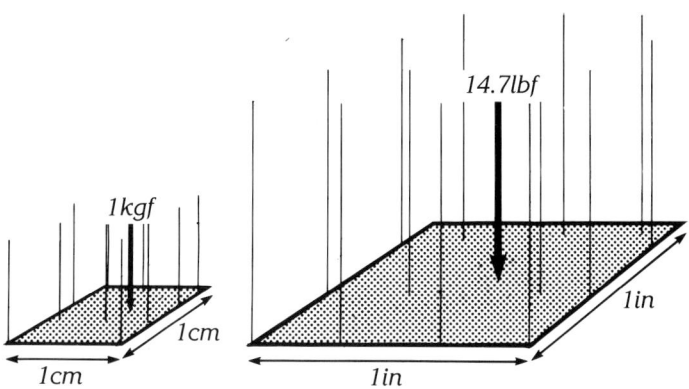

Around about the time of Torricelli's experiments an English chemist and natural philosopher called Robert Boyle was studying in Italy and had access to the writings of both Galileo and Torricelli. On his return to England he followed up the experiments, confirming the deductions of Torricelli concerning the vacuum and the fact that the mercury column was supported by the pressure of the atmosphere.

Boyle went on to develop a practical barometer by the introduction of a simple graduated scale known as a register plate. These primitive instruments were called 'baroscopes' and their main use seemed to be in measuring heights above sea level.

Liquids are very difficult to compress and pressure exerted upon them is transmitted equally throughout the body of the liquid . . . It is known as "Hydrostatic pressure"

Meanwhile, as Boyle conducted his experiments in England a famous French scientist called Blaise Pascal was also constructing mercury barometers and using them in a series of investigations, especially in terms of measuring the variation of air pressure with increase in height.

As a result of his studies Pascal invented not only the syringe but also the hydraulic press, and it is worth remembering his very important contribution to the early study of the effects of pressure, especially on fluids, because his name will occur later when we look at modern units of pressure.

The early use of the barometer to measure height was a technique which was taken to greater accuracy some two hundred years later when aircraft were invented and the altimeter was developed.

*   *   *

CHAPTER TWO

The barometer and the weather — in the beginning. . . .

In the early stage of development the connection between the type of weather pattern and the height of the mercury in the column had not been noted.

However, it was not long before attempts were made to correlate the height of the mercury with the prevailing weather.

This resulted in the introduction of the general descriptions that are to be found marked on the height scale, words such as 'Fair', 'Changeable', 'Rain' and 'Stormy', which are still in use even today.

The barometer as an instrument for use in weather forecasting had arrived.

In 1645 the Royal Society of London designed its own barometer, but it was not for another 25 years that a domestic use for the instrument was recognised.

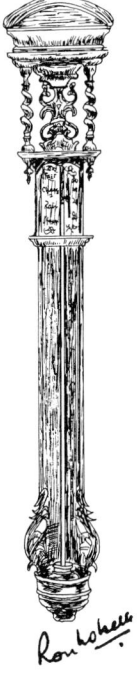

The early versions were usually made by clockmakers and one of the first of the craftsmen was a certain John Patrick who became known as the 'Torricellian Operator', presumably because all the instruments he constructed were all of the 'open cistern' type.

During the next century barometers became increasingly popular. Each was fitted with a decorative brass or metal plate, inscribed with a scale and heavily polished to avoid the need for regular cleaning.

However, they did have the disadvantage of being difficult to move from place to place. They had to be carried carefully, with concern for the position of both the glass tube and the reservoir of mercury in the cistern. Displacement of the tube from the vertical could allow air to seep in, thus reducing the vacuum and giving false readings. Also any rapid inclination often resulted in the mercury rising inside the tube with sufficient force to break the glass.

Example of an early "open cistern" barometer

Various methods were introduced to remedy these problems, such as covering the open top of the cistern with soft leather which, whilst allowing air to permeate, did offer some protection to the mercury.

The damage associated with the upwards surge of mercury was partly solved by constricting the bore of the tube in the top few inches.

The final solution which made the barometer truly portable appeared around 1695 and is attributed to Daniel Quare who was awarded the patent.

In Quare's design the mercury reservoir was contained in a leather bag which was supported inside a closed cistern. The mouth of the bag was firmly sealed to the glass tube and its base was resting on a padded screw. The screw was operated through the bottom of the cistern box and when it was moved upwards it reduced the volume of the leather bag to the point where the cistern and tube were filled of mercury.

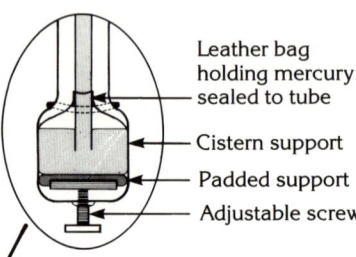

Leather bag
holding mercury
sealed to tube

Cistern support

Padded support

Adjustable screw

In this position the barometer could be inverted without any danger.

These important developments meant that the barometer suddenly had a much greater range of use, especially in relation to sea going operations.

Even in these very early days the emphasis seemed to be on making them attractive as well as functional. The wooden frames originally designed as protection for the glass tube assumed another function as they became increasingly ornate so that they would blend with other items of furniture, which is what the barometer tended to become.

It is only in this respect that there is some resemblance with today's instrument.

The barometer proliferated and various designs emerged which attempted to overcome some of the other disadvantages of the open cistern mercury in glass instrument.

Since the extremes of atmospheric pressure meant that the height of the column only altered by about 7.5cm(3in) maximum, it was considered desirable to try and extend the scale.

One simple way of achieving this was to bend the tube at a height of about 68cm(27in) above the level of the mercury in the cistern.

These 'Angle Tube' barometers suffered from the fact that the shape of the mercury meniscus varied depending upon whether the pressure was falling or rising, and this seriously impaired their accuracy.

Also they did tend to look very unsightly and so did not become popular.

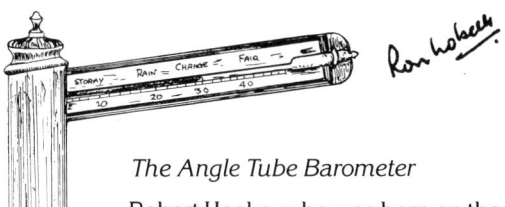

The Angle Tube Barometer

Robert Hooke, who was born on the Isle of Wight, was responsible for the invention of one other form of early barometer known as the 'Wheel Barometer'.

It was designed in an attempt to increase the accuracy by extending the scale.

A form of siphon tube it relies upon changes in the height of the mercury in the short arm to record the pressure.

A float is connected to a pulley which rotated a pointer over the face of a circular scale and greatly amplified any movement.

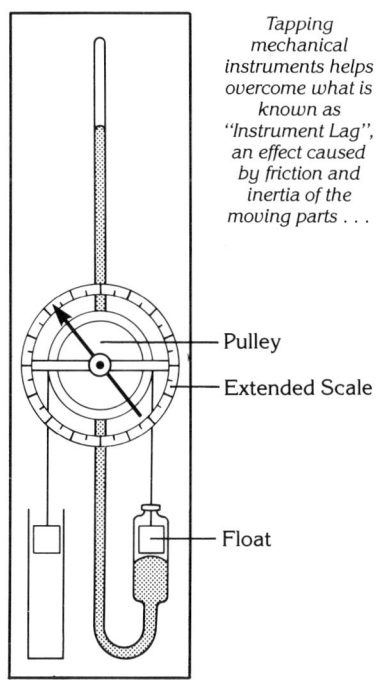

Tapping mechanical instruments helps overcome what is known as "Instrument Lag", an effect caused by friction and inertia of the moving parts . . .

Pulley

Extended Scale

Float

Robert Hooke's Wheel Barometer

The device never became a recognised scientific instrument but the circular design meant that it could be made to look very attractive, rather like a clock, and for this reason alone they became popular in the domestic market.

They did have one advantage in that the needle often responded to a sharp 'Tap' thus bringing the reading up to date and giving a quick indication of whether the pressure was rising or falling. Tapping the barometer is very much in fashion to this day.

Although water is not a satisfactory liquid for use in a barometer, some early instruments did make use of it and these were known as "Weather Glasses".

Invented well before Torricelli carried out his experiments using mercury the weather glass is a primitive form of barometer.

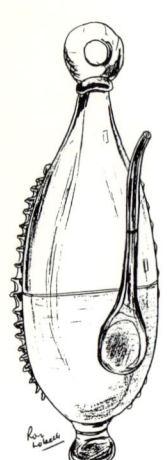

Dutch weather glass

The best known type is the Dutch Weather Glass which in Holland is called the "Donderglas" or Thunderglass since thunderstorms could be expected if water dripped from the spout.

They were prepared by immersing the vessel in water, then, by careful heating, the amount of air and hence water in the reservoir could be adjusted so that it was about half full at normal atmospheric pressure and temperature.

In this form the glass responds to changes in the air pressure for example when it decreases water rises in the spout and eventually drips out, whereas rising pressure forces the level in the spout to fall.

Obviously the weather glass is very temperature dependent since marked changes will affect not only the volume of air trapped in the glass, but also the vapour pressure of the water, which if it increases will force water upwards in the spout, even if the external air pressure is not falling.

The above temperature effects will occur notwithstanding the straightforward contraction and expansion of the water column in the spout.

The most extreme responses take place when the air temperature is low and the pressure is high which causes contraction. Alternatively, high temperature combined with low pressure brings about excessive expansion. Perhaps to the extent that water is extruded from the spout.

These latter conditions, of high temperature and low pressure are often those associated with the development of summer thunderstorms, which explains the Dutch name for the Weather Glass.

Thus it is essential that the device be kept at as near constant temperature as possible.

At this stage it is worth looking at some of the other discoveries and inventions of Robert Boyle and how they have been developed to produce some of the modern machines that we take for granted.

When Boyle was at Oxford, together with Robert Hooke, he constructed an air pump. This device enabled him to carry out further studies and experiments upon the air which eventually lead to his famous discovery now known as 'Boyles Law'.

This simple mathematical equation showed that if you had a fixed volume of a gas at constant temperature and you compressed the gas, then the temperature increased. Conversely, causing the gas to expand lowered its temperature.

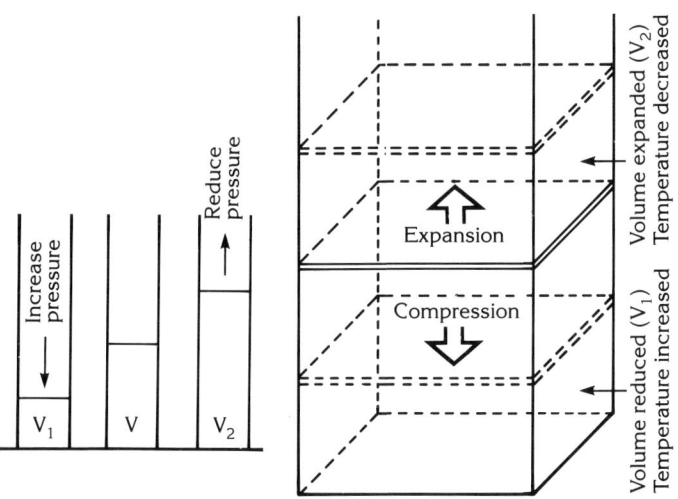

If you have ever had to pump up a bicycle tyre then you will have experienced the compression/heating effect. Each time the air in the pump is compressed before it passes through the valve into the tyre, it is heated slightly and some of the heat is transferred to the barrel of the pump. Over a long period and with many repeated compressions the heat builds up and the pump's barrel can become quite hot.

Pressures from a tyre pressure gauge give values in excess of normal atmospheric pressure. Thus a tyre pressure of 2kg/sq.cm(28lb/ sq.in) is an absolute pressure of 3kg/sq.cm(42lb/ sq.in) . . .

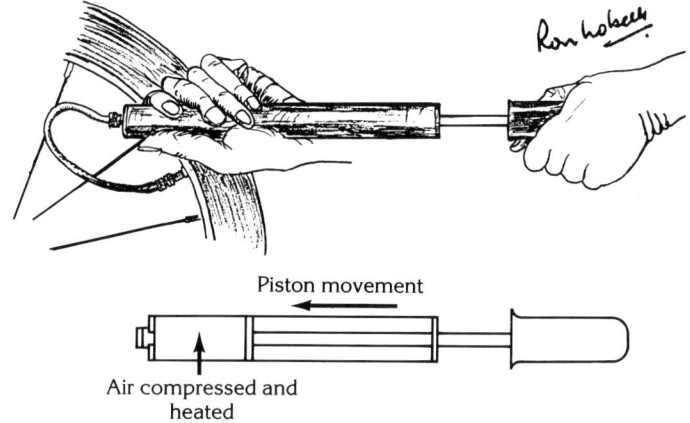

This heating effect forms the basis of the diesel engine . . .

The air contained in the cylinder is rapidly compressed by a moving piston. This causes a rise in temperature to a point where the fuel that is injected into the cylinder forms an explosive mixture, forcing the piston back. A system of valves controls the removal of combustion products and the introduction of fresh air, whilst the continual movement of the piston is translated into a driving force.

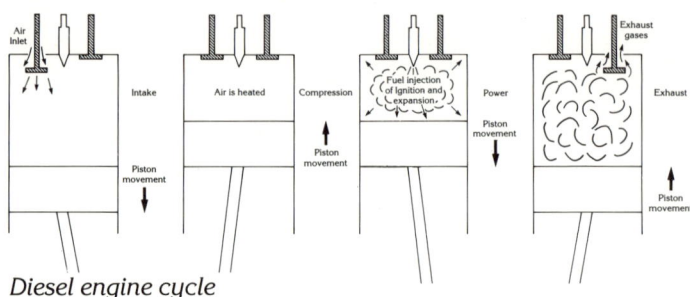

In a petrol engine ignition of the fuel mixture is caused by a spark plug . . .

Diesel engine cycle

The cooling effect caused by the forced expansion of a gas can be used for refrigeration.

The first refrigerator was invented by Jacob Perkins in 1834 . . .

A gas is compressed and then forced through a nozzle into a large chamber where it expands rapidly. This rapid expansion lowers the temperature and with the correct design the cooling can be increased each time.

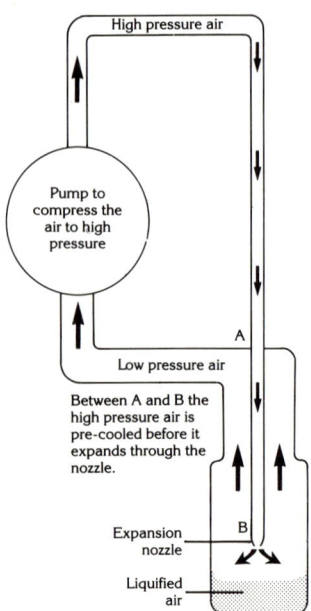

This technique is used to produce liquid air.

Actually in the modern 'fridge the process used to lower the temperature also depends upon the cooling effect of evaporation. Which is the way a liquid changes into a gas without reaching its boiling point.

If you lick the back of your hand and blow across it, you will notice that the wet area feels cold. This is because the water on your hand takes heat from your hand as it evaporates to form water vapour.

In the 'fridge a liquid that has a low boiling point is pumped around the system under high pressure and then forced into a chamber where it expands. The sudden drop in pressure causes the liquid to change into a gas by the process of evaporation, and this takes heat from inside the 'fridge. The gas is then compressed back to liquid and recycled.

In terms of weather processes, both evaporation with its requirement for heat, and the opposite effect condensation which involves a release of heat, are very important. The liquid involved is, of course, water.

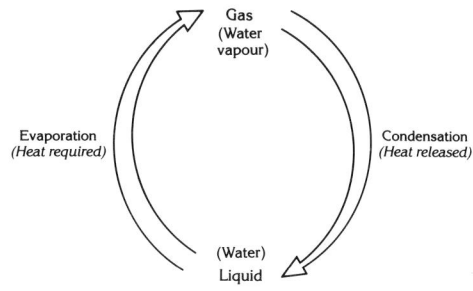

The heat required to cause evaporation comes from the sun, which heats the Earth's surface to a much greater degree than it heats the atmosphere.

The land heats up, and cools down, very quickly whereas the oceans respond much more slowly but do store a lot more heat.

As a result they provide large quantities of water vapour to the atmosphere, especially over the equatorial and tropical oceans.

This water vapour eventually condenses to form clouds which give precipitation in the form of rain or snow which in turn finds its way to the oceans.

This is the so called "Water Cycle".

In a dry climate under clear skies, water in a shallow earthenware tray, set upon straw, cools sufficienty due to evaporation to form ice . . .

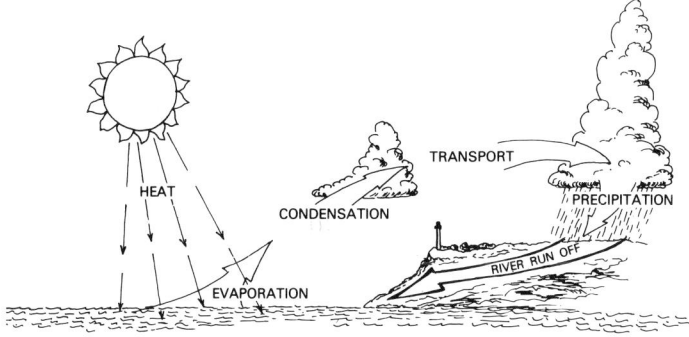

In fact one could say that if there is no water or water vapour available then there is no "weather" in the form we recognise.

Evaporation also occurs when hot dry air flows over a cooler sea, and when cold dry air contacts a warmer sea . . .

Another important feature of the atmosphere is also explained by Boyle's Law and that is the decrease in pressure with increase in height.

If you consider that the pressure at sea level is the result of the weight of the column of air pressing on unit area, then at the top of a mountain the column of air above the point has less weight, therefore the pressure is less.

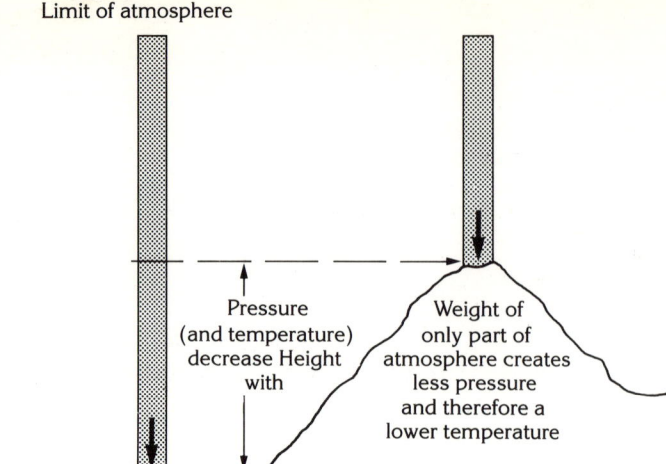

Limit of atmosphere

Pressure (and temperature) decrease Height with

Weight of only part of atmosphere creates less pressure and therefore a lower temperature

The limit of the atmosphere in which the weather processes take place is called the Tropopause . . .

Weight of complete atmosphere creates pressure at sea level

Since the pressure has decreased, but the volume has remained sensibly constant, the temperature is also lowered.

Which is what we find in a normal atmosphere: both temperature and pressure decrease with increase in height.

The fall in temperature with height is called the "Lapse Rate" and there are two values. For dry air the temperature decrease with increase in height is 3C per1000ft and this is known as the Dry Adiabetic Lapse Rate (DALR).

Thus, if the dry air temperature at the surface is 21C, then at 7000ft it will be 0C ie freezing point.

For air that contains water vapour the rate of cooling is not constant and for practical purposes it is taken as 1.5C per 1000ft. This is the Saturated Adiabatic Lapse Rate(SALR).

Thus for foggy air, saturated with water vapour, if the temperature is 12C at the surface then, if the fog extends to 2000ft, the temperature at that height will have fallen to about 9C.

Depending upon the prevailing pressure pattern the variation of temperature with height can show some anomalous properties as we shall see later.

CHAPTER THREE

Another famous name associated with mercury barometers is that of Admiral Fitzroy, who lived in the 19th century.

Robert Fitzroy was the naval officer who in fact commanded HMS Beagle, the ship that took Charles Darwin on his great voyage of discovery.

Fitzroy had a great interest in the developing science of meteorology and after his retirement he devoted himself to the subject.

His work included the introduction of a system for warning mariners of impending storms, which was an early form of the weather forecast.

However, nowadays he is most famous for the invention of the specialised barometer that bears his name.

Marine barometers of the period were too delicate for general usage amongst seafarers. Fitzroy from experience knew that they were difficult to read and that any discharge of the ship's guns often caused them to shatter.

He therefore made it his task to design a barometer that would not suffer from these faults and came up with the following solutions:

. . . *the case was made of brass and therefore was not liable to rust like the original iron cased instrument . . .*

. . . *the glass tube containing the mercury was packed in a sheath of rubber which protected it from vibration and external shocks . . .*

. . . *the scale was made of porcelain, which was easily read . . .*

. . . *each part of the barometer could be dismantled and cleaned . . .*

Fitzroy was also very concerned that not only should those at sea have access to the barometer but also that those who were contemplating setting sail should also have the opportunity to consult one. He persuaded the Board of Trade to provide what was known as a 'Fishery or Sea Coast' barometer in many villages and towns around the shores of England. These instruments, set as they were in prominent positions, were also supplied by the Royal National Lifeboat Institution, and there is little doubt that those who learned to read them often avoided the sudden changes in weather that cost lives at sea.

From his studies Fitzroy discovered that the standard words such as 'Fair', 'Changeable', 'Stormy' etc. had little or no bearing upon what the weather pattern was likely to be. He realised that the most important factor was not the actual height of the mercury but rather the rise or fall in the height of the column, but even this on its own was only a part of the story.

The speed and direction of the wind, plus the humidity of the air were also very important, and had to be considered when preparing any weather forecast.

Consequently he designed a scale which took into account these other factors and allowed a much more sensible and useful estimation of forthcoming weather.

For the first time the barometer was making a significant contribution to weather forecasting.

Admiral Fitzroy went further and set up a series of weather reporting stations which were part of a Storm warning service.

The stations were all connected to a central office in London by the newly invented telegraph system and sent in their data on a regular basis.

The information was used to plot the first 'weather charts', on which the forecasts were based.

The result of this pioneering work meant that Fitzroy gained great recognition as a weather forecaster, to the extent that 'The Times' published his charts and forecasts on a daily basis from 1860.

But his work was not without controversy and as a result of the pressures from scientific opponents he took his life in 1865.

It was after his death that the so called 'Admiral Fitzroy barometer' became available in large numbers.

Its popularity was undoubtedly due to the fact that it was the first to be mass produced, notwithstanding the detailed descriptions of probable weather conditions that adorned the scale, and became known as 'Admiral Fitzroy's scale words'.

In fact the design of this barometer bears no resemblance to that developed from Fitzroy's specifications, described earlier. Examination shows that they rely on the 'Siphon tube' principle, and they probably owe their name to the printed weather indications devised by Fitzroy.

These were as follows:

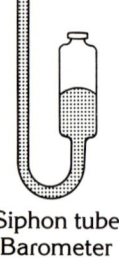

Siphon tube
Barometer

On the left hand side.... *'Rising'*

1st. A steady rising barometer which when continued shows very fine weather.

2nd. In winter the rise of the barometer presages frost.

3rd. In wet weather if the mercury rise high and remain so expect fine weather but if the mercury rise suddenly very high, fine weather will not last long.

4th. A rapid rise of the barometer indicates unsettled weather a slow movement the contrary.

On the right hand side. . . . *'Falling'*

N.B. The barometer rises highest of all for north and east wind.

1st. *If a fall take place with a rising thermometer wind and rain may be expected from the south-eastward, southward or south-westward.*

2nd. *A fall with a low thermometer foretells snow or rain.*

3rd. *A sudden fall of the barometer with westerly winds is generally followed by a violent storm from the NW or NE.*

4th. *A rapid fall indicates wind or wind and rain.*

5th. *In very hot weather the fall of the mercury denotes thunder, or a sudden fall indicates high wind.*

Indications of approaching changes are shewn less by the height of the barometer than by the falling or rising. Thus the figures are of more importance than the words. The mercury falls lowest for wind and rain together, next to that for wind, except it be an east or northeast wind.

The barometer also contains what is known as the *'Mountain Scale'* described as follows:

Air being a substance possessing gravity it necessarily presses downwards in the direction of the centre of the earth and therefore the degree of pressure on any given point will be equal to the column of air above that point and proportional to its density. The atmosphere is of the greatest vertical height at the level of the sea and here its pressure is about 15 pounds on every square inch of surface, which pressure is exerted in every direction.

The atmosphere which envelopes the earth on every side extends to a height of about forty five-miles, diminishing in density from the sea level upwards. In the diagram is a representation of the atmosphere divided by horizontal lines into thirty spaces each containing an equal quantity of air. The lower layers however are so greatly compressed by the weight of those above them that the lower half of the atmosphere lies within four miles of the sea level, while the upper half is so much expanded as to occupy upwards of forty miles.

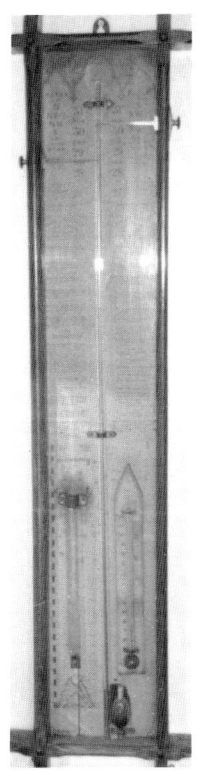

Fitzroy's Barometer

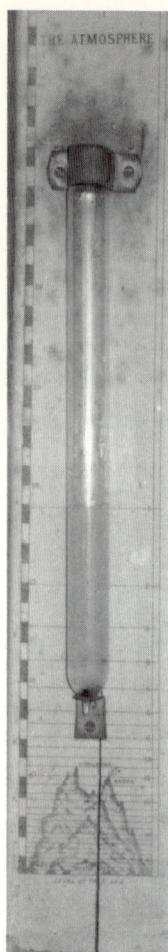

"Storm Glass"

Another instrument used for foretelling the weather and found on the Fitzroy barometer is the "Storm Glass", sometimes known as a "Chemical Weather Glass".

The origins of this device are obscure but it certainly has been in existence for over 200 years.

It consists of a simple glass bottle about 25cm(10in) long which is hermetically sealed. Inside the bottle is a solution of various compounds in aqueous alcohol.

There are various combinations of the constituents, but one formula that appears to be successful is the following:

Dissolve 150g of Camphor in 20ml of alcohol. Take 15ml of water and dissolve in it 30g of Potassium Nitrate followed by 35g of Ammonium Chloride.

Add the camphor solution slowly to the aqueous solution with constant stirring.

The changes in the appearance of the solution are said to signify the weather, in that:

Clear liquid means dry and bright;
Crystals at the bottom indicate hard frost;
A turbid liquid means rain, but with small stars then thunder;
Large flakes in winter then snow is likely;
Fine threads in the upper part of the solution predicts windy weather;
Small dots suggest fog and drizzle;
Small stars on bright days in winter then expect snow in the next couple of days;

It is suggested that in winter the higher the crystals rise up inside the glass the colder it will become.

The solubility of the chemicals must vary with the air temperature. Thus, when it is cold more crystals will be deposited, which gives some idea of how the "Weather Glass" worked.

In a modern centrally heated house I wonder if it would show any changes at all . . .?

CHAPTER FOUR

Aneroid Barometers

Modern barometers are nothing like the classic mercury barometer, as anyone who has one will appreciate.

Their operation depends on the movement of what is known as an aneroid capsule. The word aneroid means 'without liquid', and this is what gives this type of instrument its versatility.

Aneroid capsules were invented in 1843 by a Frenchman called Lucien Vidie, who was a steam engineer.

Through his studies into ways of recording steam pressure, and following on work carried out by another Frenchman Eugene Bourdon, Vidie constructed a metal box which was partially exhausted of air, and then sealed.

The Bourdon tube gauge invented in 1850 is still widely used today for measuring very high pressures in liquids and gases . . .

The top and bottom of the box were corrugated in concentric circles which made them very flexible.

By fixing the lower surface and supporting the upper by a spring, any change in atmospheric pressure caused the box to expand or contract.

The movement is detected and amplified by a system of levers connected to a pointer, which moves over a calibrated scale.

Since the whole instrument is built of metal it is very robust and easily transportable. Another important point is the fact that not only could the size be reduced when compared to the clumsy mercury barometers, but the essential parts were easily mass produced by machines.

The result was that the introduction of the aneroid barometer meant the virtual end of the very expensive and difficult to transport mercury barometer.

Admiral Fitzroy immediately recognised their potential and suggested improvements to the lever system. He also designed a means of compensating for temperature changes, which could have a significant effect upon the metal parts, and hence the accuracy.

As a result the marine version became of great benefit to the sea faring community, since it did not suffer the 'pumping' sometimes developed by mercury barometers in high seas.

These marine instruments were about 12cm(4.5in) in diameter and 5cm(2in) in thickness, similar to today's version.

In the 1860's a pocket aneroid barometer was developed which found its main use in altitude measurements, although miners also made reference to them in order to determine the depth of shafts.

So far we have looked at the readings obtained from the various types of barometer in terms of the 'Height of Mercury' and this has been expressed in either Centimetres or Inches.

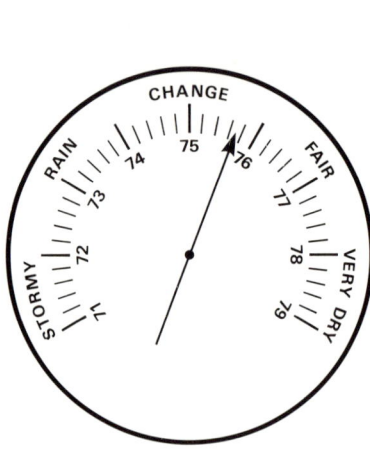

Barometer dial calibrated in
"Centimetres of Mercury"
(Actual Reading = 75.7 cm. of Hg.)

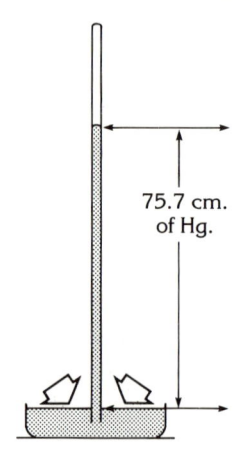

75.7 cm. of Hg.

Atmospheric Pressure
would support a
column of mercury (Hg) to
the height shown.

We have also considered atmospheric pressure in terms of 'Weight per unit area', which can be changed to 'Force per unit area' since 'weight' is a form of 'force'.

Pressures less than atmospheric are negative gauge pressures and are thought of in terms of "partial vacuum" or "suction" since they are measured from a gauge pressure of zero . . .

The units mentioned were 'Kilogram per square centimetre' and 'Pounds per square inch', neither of which are particularly useful when it comes to measuring the small changes that can occur in atmospheric pressure.

Therefore, to avoid difficulties, a unit of pressure was introduced called the 'Millibar', and most modern aneroid barometers have scales marked in 'Millibars'.

They also tend to have the old fashioned scale marked in 'Inches of Mercury' or in some cases, if the barometer was built on the continent, 'Centimetres of Mercury'.

Now, if pressure is related to 'weight' then gravity is involved (the weight of a body depends on gravity for example the weight of a man is reduced when he is on the moon's surface because the gravity of the moon is about $1/6$th that on Earth)

Over the surface of the Earth there is a variation in the effect of gravity, it is greater at the poles than at the equator.

Which means that the pressure can vary simply due to the effects of local gravity, and corrections have to be applied to the readings of mercury barometers to compensate for this effect as we shall see in an example later.(p.32)

It may be that you will come across a unit of pressure called the 'Hectopascal' (hPa). This is exactly the same as the millibar and the name has been introduced so that Blaise Pascal the Frenchman who did original work on the development of the barometer should have some form of recognition. Both units are likely to be used especially in the scientific papers, and eventually it is expected that the millibar will be phased out.

Conversions

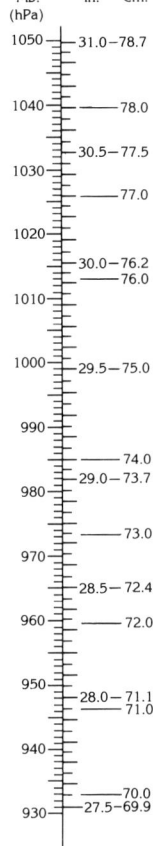

Comparison of Pressure Units

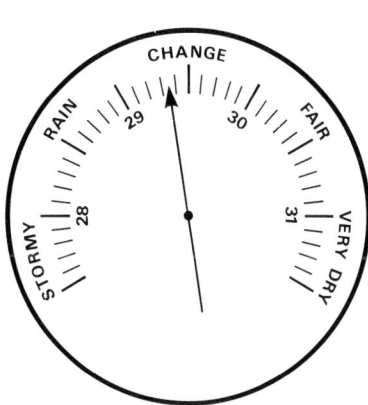

Barometer dial calibrated in
"Inches of Mercury"
(Actual Reading = 29.35 in. of Hg.)

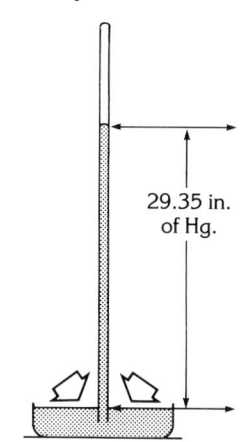

29.35 in. of Hg.

Atmospheric Pressure
will support a
column of mercury (Hg) to
the height shown.

Conversion Factors

To convert from inches of mercury to millibars:
Multiply by 33.87
eg   30.0in x 33.87 = 1016.1mb
To convert centimetres of mercury to millibars:
Multiply by 13.33
eg   76.2cm x 13.33 = 1016.1mb

Alternatively to convert millibars to either inches or centimetres of mercury simply divide by the appropriate figure.

23

In the introduction it was stated that the principle of the barometer was the most important discovery in meteorology.

From this, one might be tempted to conclude that atmospheric pressure is the single most important piece of information.

This is not the case and, as we know, Fitzroy recognised that it is the change in pressure that is vital, not the actual reading.

In order to get the best from your barometer it is useful to understand how pressure is used in the preparation of the weather forecast.

Understanding how the data is gathered and how a forecast is prepared will help in recognising the uncertainties that inevitably exist . . . in other words how accurate the forecast is likely to be and how quickly it might start to go wrong . . . this is where the barometer will be most valuable . . . especially when used in conjunction with other weather related factors . . .

CHAPTER FIVE

The barometer and surface pressure patterns

The barometer not only measures air pressure at any point on the Earth's surface but using the information on a regular basis further simple but very important calculations can be made. These, when considered together with other meteorological data, can have an important input into the preparation of a weather forecast.

A weather forecast depends upon accurate weather observations. These are gathered every hour, 24 hours a day, 365 days a year, from observing stations sited all over the world.

It is not just on land that data is collected. Ships on passage also make hourly reports, as do those specialised 'Weather ships' tasked to maintain position in a particular area of the ocean.

A weather observation contains several different measurements and calculations and usually includes the following main data.

(Note: the list is not exhaustive nor in any order of importance and it refers to readings taken 'at the time of observation').

Air temperature (measured in degrees Celsius($^\circ$C))

Dew Point — this is calculated. It is the temperature to which the air must be cooled in order to cause any water vapour it contains to condense into water droplets. In foggy conditions the Air temperature and Dew point should be the same. If the air is very dry then the Dew point will probably be several degrees below the Air Temperature.

Wind Speed — measured in knots.

Wind Direction — from which it is blowing. (Note: Both speed and direction are usually measured at a height of 10m(33ft)).

Prevailing 'Weather' which means . . . is it . . . raining . . . snowing . . . foggy . . . thunderstorms . . . sleet . . . etc . . .?

Past Weather — what has happened in the hour since the last observation? Has it . . . rained . . . snowed . . . etc?

Visibility — at the surface, measured horizontally (metres or km).

Amount of sky covered by cloud — measured in 'oktas' or 'eights' eg ^{4}/$_8$ means half the sky covered by cloud.

Types of cloud and their height — these are subdivided into 'Low level', 'Medium level' and 'High level'.

Surface pressure — Measured using the barometer (millibars).

Pressure tendency — The amount the barometric reading has changed over the last three hours. This is a very important parameter as we shall see.

1 Knot (kt) is 1 nautical mile per hour. A nautical mile is 1852 metres (6076.12 feet). Wind speeds are also measured in metres per second (m/sec).

Thus you can see that even in one single weather observation there is a remarkable amount of information and remember this procedure is taking place all over the world: *every hour; 24 hours a day; 365 days of the year* . . . and so represents a tremendous volume of data . . . in other words, an awful lot of weather . . . !

One of the interesting points about this weather data is that it is gathered in all the countries that comprise the world community at almost exactly the same time each hour.

Also, and very importantly, the information is freely exchanged, between all nations...in times of peace that is . . .

When you think about this global co-operation it is quite amazing and heartwarming to realise that all the artificial barriers that men erect between themselves do not matter.

Observations are always taken at Greenwich Mean Time (GMT). Thus, it may be 10 p.m. local time in Sydney, Australia, but the weather observation is recorded as 1200 GMT.

Divisive issues, such as attitudes in religion and politics which are very much man made concepts, are irrelevant. Even the more obvious but equally insignificant differences like colour of skin, written or spoken languages, and 'national character', are all put aside for the happy exchange of weather data. Remembering that the information is gathered at almost exactly the same time worldwide, it is sobering to realise that Men and Women; Hindu and Moslem; Jew and Christian; Catholic and Protestant; Communist and Democrat; Conservative and Labourite; White, Red, Yellow, Brown and Black skinned people are all actively engaged in a common task, for a common cause.

I know of no other field of human activity that regularly and repeatedly unites the planet in this way.

The 'Weather' does . . .

The reasons are obvious, whatever our colour, creed or political persuasion we all have to suffer or enjoy the weather. Despite our perception of our ability to alter or affect the atmosphere, we are still a very long way from having any significant effect upon the random, day to day fluctuations that go to make up . . . 'the weather'.

Obviously there are many different languages on Earth both spoken and written and in order to make use of all the hourly data that is collected it is vital that everyone can understand exactly what the weather is doing all over the globe.

This communication problem is overcome by use of a numerical code. Thus, English speakers can readily understand the weather data from China, where not only is the spoken language different but the written word is as well. This applies to all Nations, and so total understanding of weather data exists.

CODED WEATHER MESSAGE

03776 41459 61515 10090 20071 40025 58010 76081 84872
333 84625 84360

Meaning:

03	Observation from UK/Eire
776	London/Gatwick

4	No rainfall reported
1	Significant weather reported — (7-group)
4	Code figure for height of low cloud
59	Horizontal visibility

6	Total amount of sky covered in cloud
15	Wind direction: from 150 degrees
15	Wind speed in kt.

1	Indicator figure: Air Temp follows.
0	Air Temp is plus. (If = 1 Air Temp is minus)
090	Air temp = +09.0C

2	Indicator figure: Dew Pt Follows.
0	Dew Pt is plus. (If = 1 Dew Pt is minus)
071	Dew pt = +07.1C.

4	Indicator figure: Sea level pressure follows.
0025	Pressure = 1002.5mb corrected to sea level.

5	Indicator figure: Barometric tendency follows.
8	Barometer is falling (see table p 41).
010	Pressure has fallen 1mb in last 3 hrs.

7	Indicator figure: significant weather follows.
60	Weather at time of observation (Light intermittent rain)
8	Showers in past 6 hours.
1	No other significant past weather.

8	Indicator figure: Cloud information follows.
4	Total of low cloud of type given next:
8	Low cloud type: Stratocumulus & Cumulus.
7	Medium level cloud type: Altocumulus.
2	High level cloud type: Cirrus.

333	Indicator group for extra regional data.

8	Indicator figure: More detailed cloud data.
3	Amount of cloud type.
8	Cloud type: Strocumulus/Cumulus.
25	Height of base: 2500ft.

8	Indicator: cloud data.
4	Amount of cloud type.
3	Cloud type: Altocumulus.
60	Height of base: 10,000ft.

Having solved the communication problem it is now necessary to use that data to build up a 'picture' of the weather pattern at the time of all the observations.

In order to do this the individual observations are plotted onto a map at the point where they are taken. Thus the Heathrow observation will be plotted just west of London, Paris in its appropriate place and so on for the approriate observations.

Observations are plotted according to an agreed convention, with the information displayed in the positions shown:

Not only land stations make reports but also ships on passage and specialised "Weather Ships" that maintain their position in a fixed area of ocean.

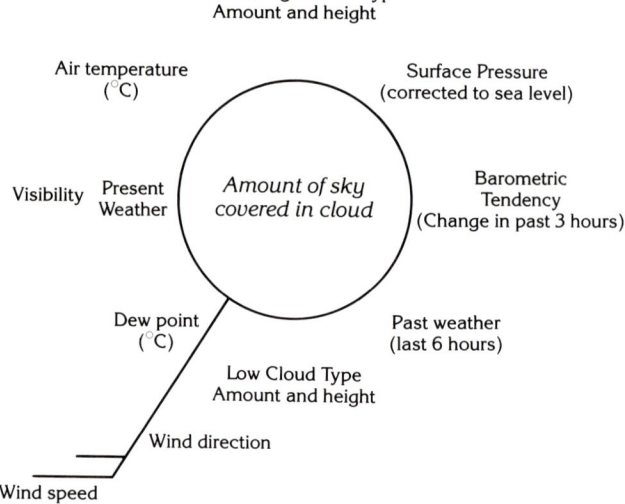

A typical plotted observation and what the data means is also shown:

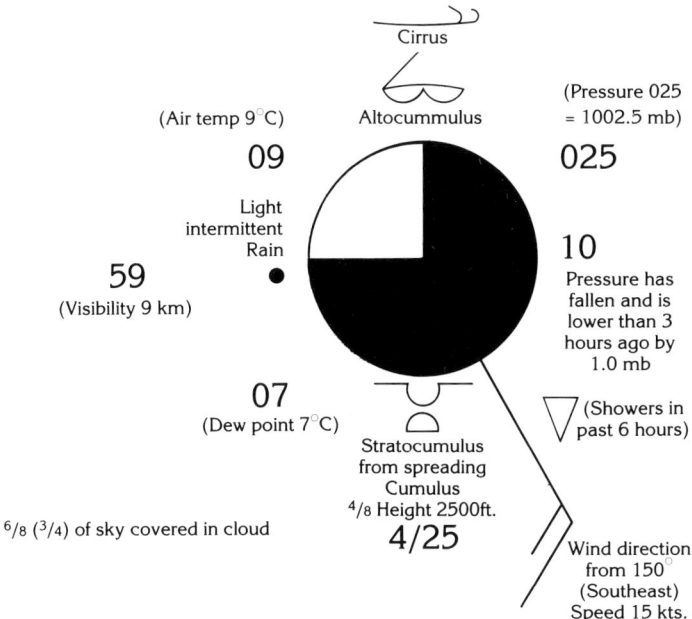

Cirrus

(Air temp 9°C)   Altocummulus

(Pressure 025 = 1002.5 mb)

09   025

Light intermittent Rain

59   •   10
(Visibility 9 km)

Pressure has fallen and is lower than 3 hours ago by 1.0 mb

07
(Dew point 7°C)

Stratocumulus from spreading Cumulus
⁴/₈ Height 2500ft.

(Showers in past 6 hours)

⁶/₈ (³/₄) of sky covered in cloud

4/25

Wind direction from 150° (Southeast) Speed 15 kts.

A few other observations are given for you to decipher . . .

To help you work out the 'weather' at the time of the observations, the following symbols refer to differing weather conditions.

WEATHER SYMBOLS *(All at the time of observation);*

•̣•   Moderate continuous rain . . .

✳ ✳   Heavy continuous snow . . .
✳

≡   Fog . . .

△
☡   Thunderstorm with hail . . .

•
✳
▽   Sleet shower . . .

•
▽   Rain shower . . .

𝟫   Light intermittent drizzle . . .

✳
▽   Heavy Snow shower . . .

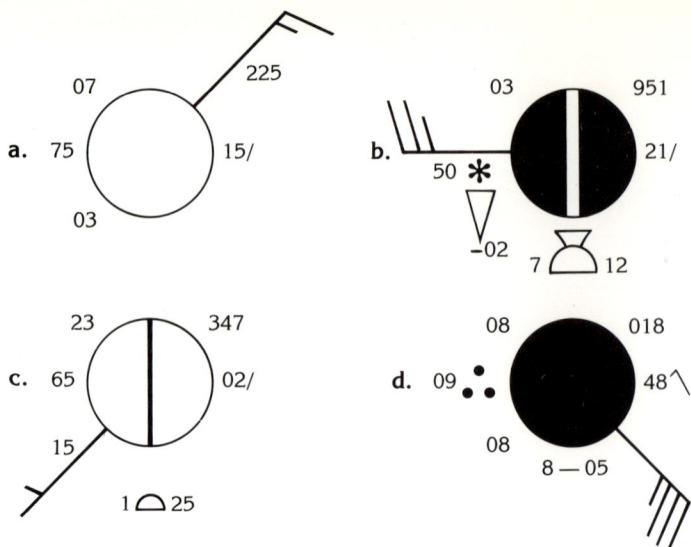

If you are unable to work out what they mean the explanations are at the bottom of the page!

Explanations:

a. No cloud; wind northeast 15 kt; Visibility 25 km; Air temp 7°C; Dew Pt. 3C Pressure 1022.5 mb; Pressure Tendency rising 1.5 mb in past 3 hours.

b. 7/8 Cloud at height 1200 ft: Cumulonimbus type; Wind westerly 25 kt; Snow shower at time of observation; Visibility 5 km; Air temp 3C; Dew pt minus 2C; Pressure 995.1 mb; Tendency rising 2.1 mb in past 3 hours.

c. 1/8 Cumulus cloud at 2500 ft; Wind southwest 5 kt; Visibility 15km; Air temp 23C; Dew Pt 15C; Pressure 1034.7 mb; Tendency rising 0.2 mb in past hours.

d. 8/8 Cloud cover: Stratus at 500 ft; Wind southeast 35 kt; Visibility 900m; Moderate continuous Rain a time of observation. Air temp 8C; Dew Pt. 8C; Pressure 1001.8 mb; Tendency falling steadily 4.8 mb in past 3 hours.

In practical terms because of limitations of space on the special maps it is not possible to plot every observation taken, so a sensible selection is made.

The maps themselves cover different areas of the Earth to different scales. For example, one may be a map that covers most of western Europe stretching out into the Eastern North Atlantic, but omitting the east coast of America.

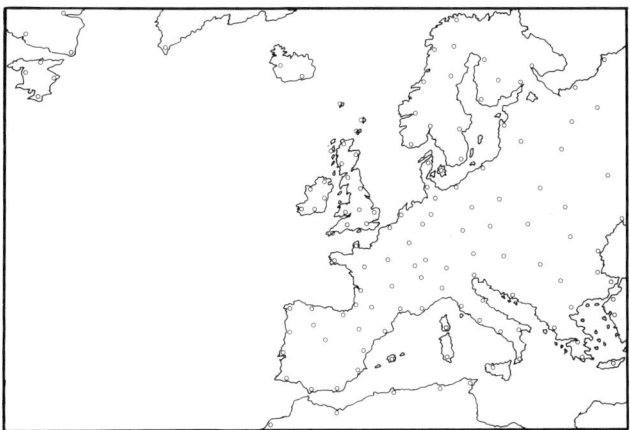

Other maps will extend to include the whole of the North Atlantic, from Greenland to the Caribbean, eastern USA to west Russian, Norway to North Africa.

The land stations are marked and ship observations are plotted from their latitude and longitude.

Now, the pressure reading used in a plotted observation is obtained from the barometer, and is the pressure at a particular point at a moment in time.

Obviously, not all the observing stations are at the same height above sea level, consequently, because pressure decreases with increase in height, the pressures reported by those at different heights cannot be immediately compared.

Therefore, it is essential to introduce some correction to the readings taken in order that the values from stations sited over a wide area of the Earth's surface can be compared.

This is done by adding a value to the actual barometer reading that takes into account the height of the observing station above mean sea level. So all reports refer to mean sea level.

For example if an observing station is 30ft above mean sea level then approximately 1mb is added to the observed pressure reading.

Similarily, if the observing station is 300ft above mean sea level then approximately 10mb is added to the actual barometer reading. (see p. 68)

The temperature of the outside air also has to be taken into account since it affects the density and hence the weight of the air.

The weight of a body varies according to gravity . . .

For mercury barometers other corrections have to be applied to allow for variations in the force of gravity over the surface of the Earth.

*The **mass** remains constant . . .*

The Earth is not perfectly spherical but is in fact flattened at the poles, rather like a tangerine. This means that gravity is greater towards the poles than at the equator. As a result of this mercury barometers at low latitudes always read high since the mercury 'weighs' less than it would at the higher latitudes. The change-over point is latitude 45 degrees north and south.

Another correction that must be applied to the mercury barometer takes account of the temperature (because the mercury expands and contracts as the temperature rises and falls) and it gives the reading that would be obtained at the standard temperature of 12C.

Finally the barometer usually has an 'index correction' which is a function of its manufacture. The value of this is determined by the National Physical Laboratory and is stated on a certificate that accompanies the instrument.

The following is an example of the correction procedure:

At Latitude 27N the reading from a mercury barometer is 1015.3mb at a height of 53ft above mean sea level. The attached thermometer reads 23C and the outside air temperature is 26C the index correction is +0.4mb

	mb
	1015.3
Index correction	+ 0.4
	1015.7
Temperature correction	− 2.3
	1013.4
Height correction (53ft at 26C)	+ 1.7
	1015.1
Gravity correction Lat 27 degrees	− 1.5
Final reading	1013.6

Reading obtained (uncorrected) 1015.3

The barometer that hangs in the hall is usually an aneroid and the sort of corrections that are essential for meteorological observing purposes do not apply.

Although the instrument is sensitive to changes in temperature the design should include a device which compensates for the effects of heat or cold on the metallic chamber.

Either of two systems could be used: one involves the use of a bimetallic strip built into the lever mechanism, whilst the other method depends on leaving a small amount of air inside the chamber.

32

Continued on page 41

Barometer set
"Fair"...
Pressure High...
shown by broken
Stratocumulus...

Falling slowly...
Increasing
Altocumulus
... warm front
approaches...

Pressure is falling
quickly...
stormy...

33

With high pressure and clear skies. . . sometimes frost, sometimes fog in Spring or Autumn.

34

*"**Cirrus:** Mares' Tails" Pressure steady. . . wind probably light. . . Increasing Cirrus warns of warm front. . . Expect pressure to start to fall. . .*

*"**Altostratus**" Barometer is falling. . . warm front near. . . rain/snow imminent. . . wind has backed and increased. . .*

Pressure steadies or starts to rise as cold front passes. . .wind veers, as heavy rain moves away. ***"Cumulonimbus"***

35

*"**Low Stratus**" forms hill fog in the warm sector,
Barometer steady. . . wind steady. . . perhaps drizzle.*

*"Summer Thunderstorm". Hot and humid . . . Barometer steady
but pressure generally "Low" . . . Expect gusts. . .*

Don't be misled by bright early mornings . . . Barometer steady or rising slowly . . .
Spring or Autumn . . . wind Northwesterly . . . Polar airstreams . . .

*Situation at 0830. . . small **Cumulus** starting to develop. . .*

Then at 1030!. . . "Get the washing indoors Mum!"

'The Great Storm'

Weather Map
3am Friday
16th October
1987

'The Storm - 25 January 1990'

Weather Map
2 pm Thursday

950 mb

39

"Mammatus"
Pressure.
generally low.
Thunderstorm
imminent. . .

Cirrostratus. . . the Halo
indicates warm front
approaching. . . expect
pressure to fall. . .

However, it is necessary to set your barometer when you first take delivery. In many cases the instructions talk about finding the height of your home above sea level, but in reality this is not necessary if you can get the equivalent sea level pressure from a Met. Office.

Once your barometer is set and provided it is within a millibar or two, it should never need readjustment.

Remember, it is not the actual pressure value that is important, it is the way in which the pressure value is changing that gives the vital clues to what is happening to the weather . . . Admiral Fitzroy recognised this simple but essential fact.

However, it must be obvious that pressure alone is only a part of the overall weather situation.

Another very important piece of information that is recorded is the way in which the pressure has altered with time.

This is called the 'Barometric Tendency' and it is a value calculated by comparing the pressure taken 3 hours previously with that at the time of the observation.

It is calculated every hour and plotted in the position shown on the (Diagram) as a value given in 'Tenths of a millibar'.

For example if the 0900GMT pressure is 1012.6mb and 3 hours later the value has fallen to 1010.2mb then the barometric tendency is 'falling, 2.4mb'

This would be plotted as: 24 with a symbol to indicate the fall. Typical symbols used are shown . . .

Pressure Tendency

Symbols used:	
Barometer higher than 3hr ago	*Barometer lower than 3hr ago*
 ⌐ Rising then falling slightly	 ⌐ Falling then rising slightly
 / Rising then levelled	 ⌐ Falling then levelled
 / Rising steadily	 \ Falling steadily
 √ Fallen, then rising steadily	 ∧ Risen, then falling steadily

Consider the following:

At 1200 (noon) the barometer reading was 1018.6mb, and by 1400(2pm) it had fallen to 1015.1mb, but at 1500(3pm) it was reading 1016.6mb.

What was the barometric tendency and which symbol should be used?

Explanation:

At 1500 the barometer is lower than 3 hours ago by an amount: (1018.6 — 1016.6) mb, that is 2mb, thus the pressure tendency is 20.

During the period the barometer has fallen to 1015.lmb and then risen to 1016.6mb thus the symbol to be used with the tendency is: "Falling then rising slightly; barometer lower than 3hr ago".

So it would be plotted as: 20 ∖

These symbols used for Pressure Tendency are derived from the shapes of the lines that are recorded on a Barograph.

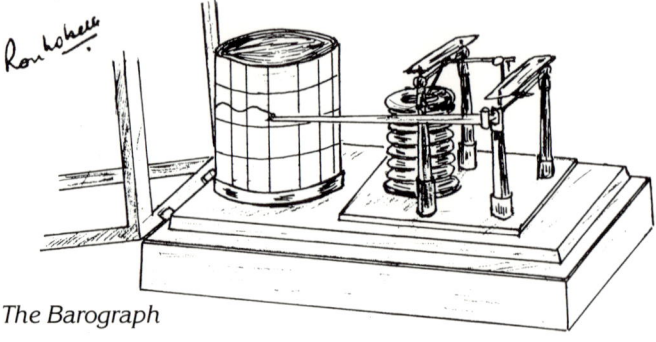

The Barograph

This is an instrument that relies on the aneroid capsule but instead of the changes being recorded by a needle moving over a scale, the variations in pressure are marked onto calibrated paper using a pen arm. In this way a continuous record of pressure against time is obtained.

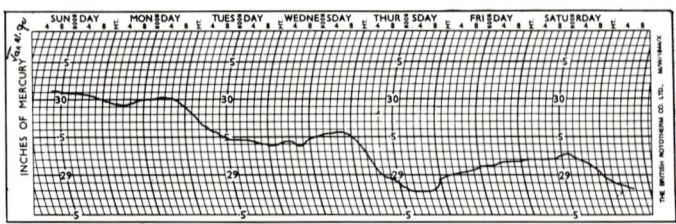

A typical trace covering one week's pressure changes is shown.

From this you can see examples of the different "Tendencies" as pressure has fallen and risen. The overall result in the example is that by the end of the week pressure had fallen considerably. This suggests a change in weather pattern from High (anticyclonic) to Low (cyclonic), with periods of rain and high winds indicated.

The value of pressure plotted on a weather chart is corrected to sea level as we have seen, and now we can take a look at how these values are used in the build up to preparing a forecast.

The diagram shows some of the many observing stations scattered across southern England and Wales, each circle represents a weather reporting station.

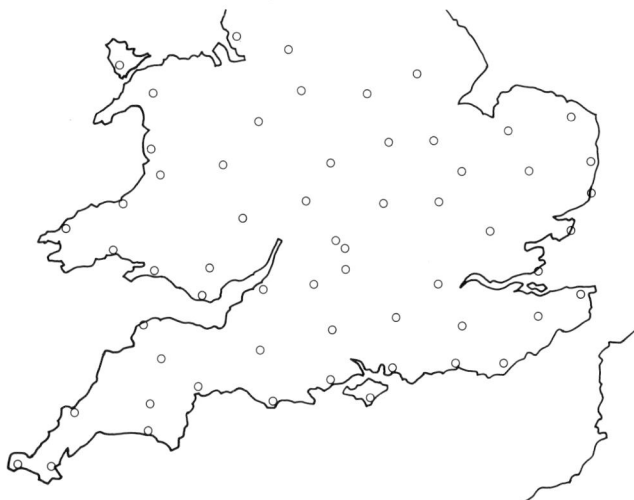

If instead of plotting the complete data around each station circle we plot only the pressure value in its appropriate place, we get a chart that looks like the following:

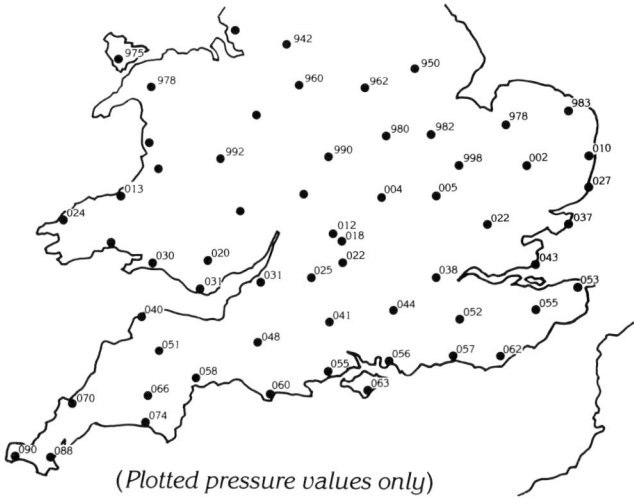

(*Plotted pressure values only*)

43

From the distribution of pressure readings we can draw in lines of equal, or almost equal, pressure.

It is not always possible to join up points of exactly equal pressure, so it is necessary to go between values that lie either side of the line we are following.

In other words we interpolate between the values plotted.

For example consider the 1000mb line. It runs across the Midlands.

In East Anglia is a plotted value of 002, which means the corrected surface pressure at the time of observation was 1000.2mb.

Further west is a plotted value of 998, which means corrected surface pressure of 999.8mb at the time of the observation.

Therefore, drawing in this 1000mb line it must go close to both these stations, with each of them on opposite sides of the line . . .

Continuing the line westwards we see that it must go between the values 004(1000.4mb) and 996(999.6mb) . . .

Similarly, looking at a line joining values close to 998mb, we see that it will run across the north of east Anglia towards north Wales . . .

Drawing in lines at 2mb spacing we build up a pattern as shown:

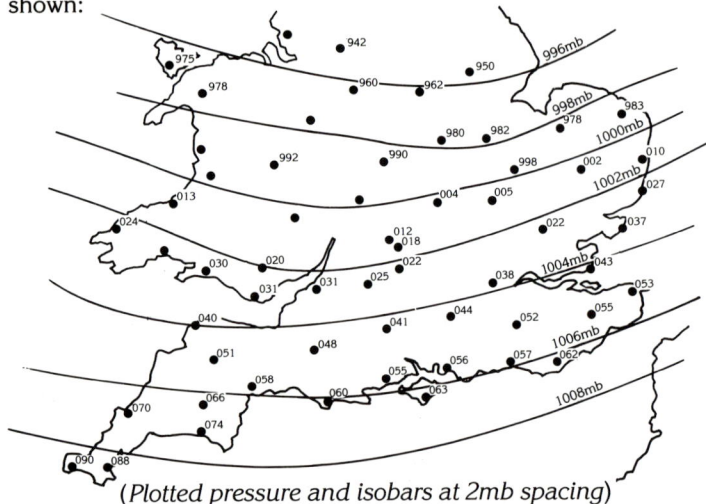

(*Plotted pressure and isobars at 2mb spacing*)

The lines of equal pressure are called 'Isobars' from the Greek: *isos* meaning equal and *baros* meaning weight.

The isobars are in effect contour lines. They are similar to those found on a map which indicate the height of the land above sea level.

In this way pressure charts are drawn and the finished product gives the centres of low and high pressure. These charts are called isobaric charts.

In the example it is obvious that lower pressure is to the north and higher pressure to the south.

Thus, we might expect to find the wind blowing from higher to lower pressure, that is from south to north.

However, if we examine the wind observations that go with the pressure readings we find that in fact the wind is blowing from just south of west to just north of east!

It is blowing almost parallel to the isobars.

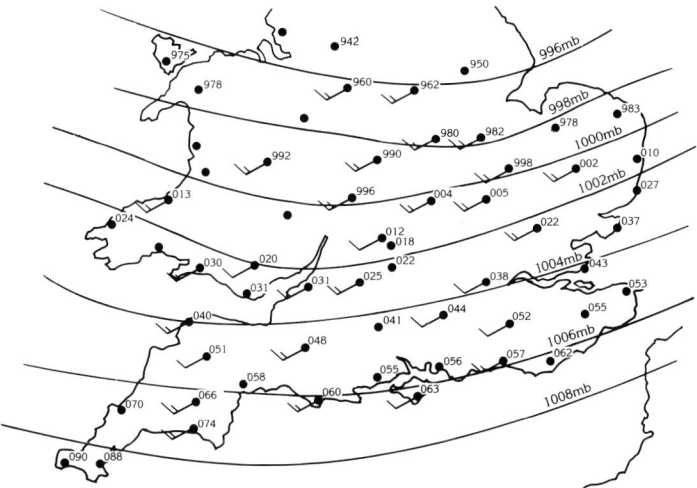

(*Plotted pressure and isobars with wind added*)

Why should this be the case? Why does the wind not blow directly from high to low pressure?

The reasons for this are to be found when a study is made of the Earth's rotation.

The Earth spins from west to east...this is why the sun rises in the east and sets in the west.

The Earth is about 25,000 miles (40,000km) in circumference around the equator and it takes 24 hours to complete one rotation about its axis.

Therefore, at the equator the Earth is moving at about 1000 mph (1600kph).

But near the Poles, through which the axis of rotation extends, the speed is very close to zero. It's a bit like a revolving gramophone record which is moving faster at the edge than near the spindle . . .

Thus across the surface of the earth from the equator to the poles there is a velocity difference, which is high at the equator dropping to nothing at the poles.

Now if a body is moving, then it will continue to move until it is either slowed or stopped by outside forces. Also, and just as important, if a body is stationary then it will remain stationary until some external force sets it into motion. This was one of Sir Isaac Newton's famous discoveries.

At certain times of the year air masses can cross the equator and as a result their curvature is reversed . . .

Thus, if you imagine an object leaving the surface of the Earth at the equator and heading for the poles it will take with it the speed of rotation and will have velocity of about 1000mph (1600kph) in an easterly direction, in addition to any velocity due to its movement polewards.

Imagine an observer at the poles whose velocity is zero watching the object come towards him...as it approaches it will curve to the observer's left, in the Northern hemisphere, but to an observer at the South Pole an object approaching from the equator curves to his right.

Now consider the movement from the viewpoint of the object as it heads polewards in the Northern hemisphere it seems to be curving to the RIGHT of its direction of motion. While in the Southern hemisphere it seems to curve to the LEFT of its direction of motion.

What this means is that all movement over the surface of the rotating Earth is curved in some way.

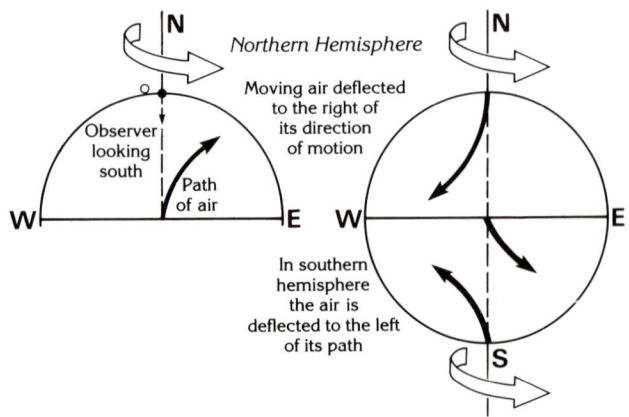

This is the reason why air does not flow in straight lines from high pressure to low, what happens is that it flows in a curved path.

You can get an idea of what is happening if you take a piece of clean paper and put a pencil at the centre. Now keeping your eyes on some distant object move the pencil in a straight line towards that object, at the same time rotate the paper with your other hand in a counterclockwise direction, that is to the left. It is important to keep your eyes on the object not the paper.

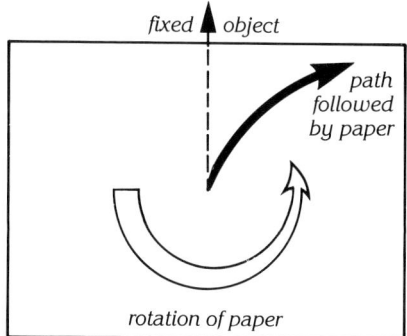

You will find that the pencil line describes a curve even though you have moved it in a straight line!

This serves to illustrate the effects of the apparent force that causes the curved movement on the surface of the Earth and which is known as the 'Coriolis Effect'.

It is related to the motion of the object, the motion of the Earth and the latitude, because the velocity of the Earth's rotation decreases with increase in latitude.

The effect is small near the equator and greater towards the poles and it always acts at right angles to the direction of motion.

Coriolis effect . . . near the equator is very small and so the wind blows across the isobars at a high angle . . .

Imagine a rocket being fired towards the UK from the equator. As it leaves the ground it will have the velocity of the Earth's rotation plus its own velocity generated by its motors.

Assume that the speed of the Earth's rotation at the latitude of the UK is about 500mph (800kph). Then at the instant the rocket leaves the ground the UK will be at a particular point in relation to the rocket. Once the rocket is airborne it starts to move to the east at a speed of 1000mph (1600kph) and at the same time the UK moves east at 500mph (800kph).

If the rocket is airborne for 6 minutes then by the time it reaches the latitude of the UK it will have moved 100 miles (160km) to the east and in the same time the UK will have moved only 50 miles (80km) eastwards, so the rocket misses by 50 miles (80km)!

Remember, the Coriolis effect applies to all movement over the surface of the Earth and it has a very significant effect upon the flight path of rockets and even aircraft, especially the very fast ones like Concorde.

It also affects the way air moves from high to low pressure, and even affects the way in which the water rotates as it disappears down the plughole!

Although to be honest because the effect upon the water movement is so small, it is the shape of the bath or basin and the plumbing that tend to dictate the rotation of the vortex.

The diagram below refers to a situation in the Northern Hemisphere and shows a high and low pressure with the lines representing pressure at a fixed distance, in other words they are isobars.

Consider air initially at rest at position (A); then let it move under the force (P) due to the difference in pressure between the high and low.

The force (P) is called the pressure gradient and its size depends on the relative values of the high and low and the distance between them. It always acts in a straight line from high to low.

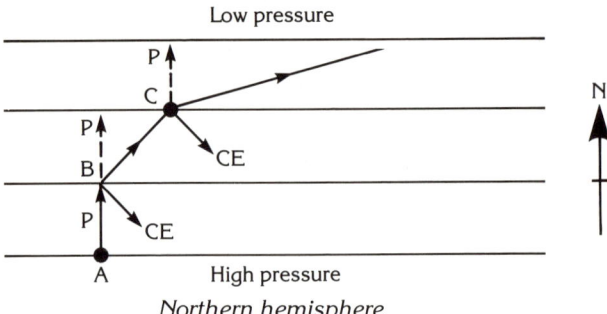

Northern hemisphere

Once the air is moving over the surface of the Earth, the Coriolis effect acts upon it, in a direction at right angles to its direction of motion.

So that after a short distance (B) the air now has two forces acting upon it, with the result it follows a new path which is not only the balance between the two, but is to the right of the direction of motion.

The new path is also subject to two forces and the result is a further move to the right.

In this way the air follows a curved path until it is eventually flowing along the lines that run between the high and low. That is: parallel to the isobars.

This result does not fit in with what we observe from the plotted wind field on page 45, which shows that the wind is blowing across the isobars, from high to low pressure.

The explanation is that close to the Earth's surface the air in motion is subjected to friction, which is generated as the air moves over the ground. (Friction is a force that occurs between all moving things.) The result of the frictional force is to reduce the wind speed near the surface and this reduces the Coriolis effect, so there is less force acting to the right, and the wind flows across the isobars.

In temperate latitudes the wind blows across the isobars at an angle between 10-15 degrees over the sea but over land the angle in-creases to between 20-30 degrees . . .

As the height increases, the friction disappears and the full Coriolis effect operates giving the situation where the wind direction parallels the pressure gradient.

It is considered that for practical purposes the wind at a height of 2,000ft and above is unaffected by friction. So by drawing in the isobars without reference to wind direction, a reasonable representation of the pressure gradient is obtained.

This means that using the isobar spacing at 2,000ft the wind speed can be calculated.

To obtain the surface wind speed from this value it is necessary to take about 70% if the air flows over the sea.

Surface Airflow over land is about 50% of that at 2000ft.

Other factors affect the surface wind such as turbulence and gusts caused by convection.

This 2000ft wind is known as the Geostrophic wind, and its speed and direction are a function of the pressure gradient and Coriolis effect only.

Wind Directions are always quoted as the direction **FROM which the wind is blowing**. . . e.g. a southerly wind comes from the south. . .

Ocean currents are always quoted as the direction **TO which the water is flowing** . . . e.g. a southerly current is moving water southwards . . .

If the isobars have a large amount of curvature then another force generates an effect. This is the so called centrifugal force, which acts on all bodies in circular motion.

This is the force that tries to throw you outwards on a roundabout.

In the atmosphere it does the same thing, so for a low pressure when the isobars have tight curvature it acts against the pressure gradient and tends to reduce wind speed.

Whereas for a high pressure with tight curvature of the isobars the centrifugal force acts with the pressure gradient to increase the wind speed.

So for the same spacing of the isobars more wind can be expected from an anticyclone than from a depression if the isobars have large curvature.

Low Pressure Cyclonic (Northern hemisphere)

Wind (W) flows in direction shown and Coriolis (CE) acts at right angles.
Centrifugal Force (CF) acts outwards which is against Pressure gradient (P)

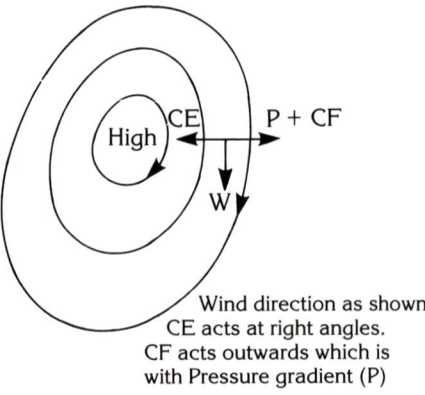

Wind direction as shown CE acts at right angles.
CF acts outwards which is with Pressure gradient (P)

CHAPTER SIX

Pressure patterns

'Is it a high or is it a low . . .?
Depends which way the wind do blow . . .!'

It is not possible to look at the barometric reading and decide what type of weather system is the cause.

This is because the actual pressure reading does not necessarily indicate whether it is caused by a low pressure system also known as a depression, or a high pressure system known as an anticyclone.

It is true to say that if the pressure value is very low then it is almost certainly a depression that is responsible. Conversely, if the pressure reading is very high, then probably an anticyclone is the main feature on the pressure map.

However, there is in between these extremes a range of pressures which could be the result of prevailing high or low pressure.

The only way you can decide is by looking at the direction of the wind, and using 'Buys-Ballot's Law'.

This states: 'If you stand with your back to the wind, then, in the Northern Hemisphere, low pressure is on your left'.

In the Northern hemisphere the air circulates around low pressure in a counter-clockwise direction . . . and around high pressure in a clockwise direction . . .

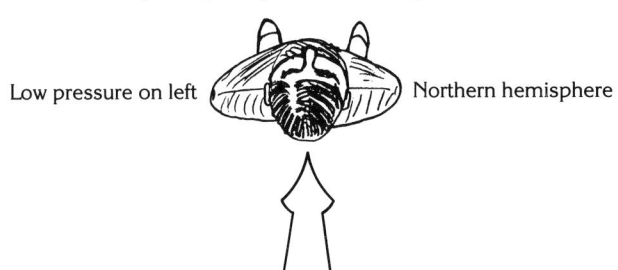

Low pressure on left   Northern hemisphere

Wind direction

For the Southern Hemisphere the opposite is true and low pressure is on the right.

The wind direction does change with time as weather systems develop.

This change is referred to as either Veering or Backing.

Surface wind flow around
Low and High pressure

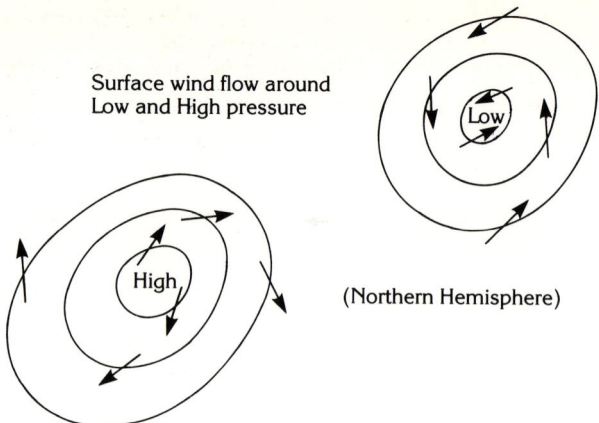

(Northern Hemisphere)

The wind is said to veer when it changes direction in a clockwise direction with time.

It backs when it goes counter clockwise . . .

The change in wind direction is often an indication of a change in the weather.

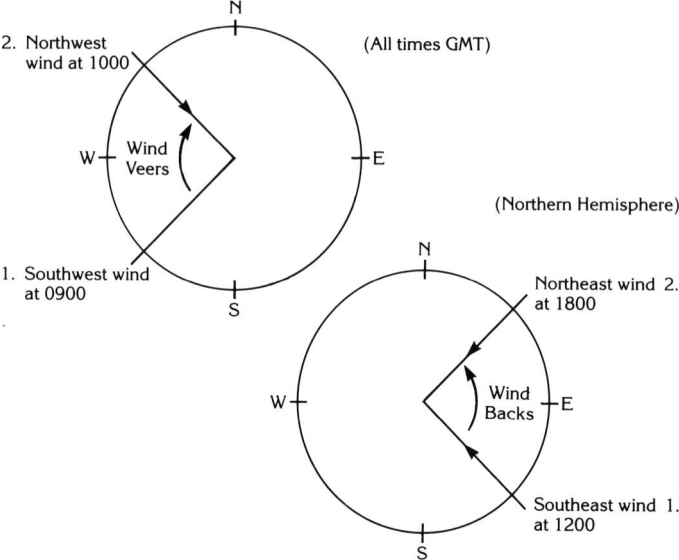

Friction has the effect of making the air flow across the isobars so that for low pressure it is spiralling towards the centre of the system. This means that at the centre the air must be rising, that is, it is acting against gravity, which is why the pressure is low!

For a high the surface air is flowing outwards from the centre, which means that it must be sinking from aloft. The sinking air acts with gravity and also compresses that beneath it giving rise to high pressure . . .

Remember the bicycle pump and the heating effect caused by compressing the air inside the barrel?

*In a low pressure air is **converging** at the surface and diverging at high altitude . . .*

*In a high pressure system air is **diverging** at the surface and converging at high altitude . . .*

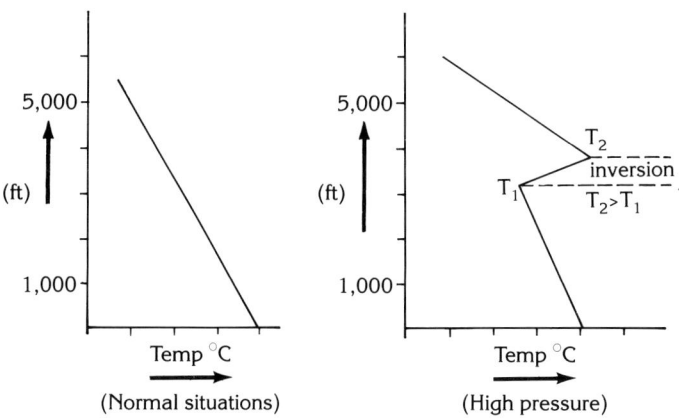

This is what happens in an anticyclone (high pressure). The sinking air compresses that in the lower levels causing a rise in temperature.

This means that instead of the temperature decreasing with increase in height, which is normal in the atmosphere, and in a low pressure centre, the situation develops where over a very small increase in height, the temperature rises.

This rise is known as a Temperature Inversion.

The inversions associated with high pressure are usually found between 2000-5000ft and can be of the order of several degrees Celsius confined to a narrow height band as little as 400ft.

53

Because they are the result of the air "sinking", they are known as "subsidence inversions" and they have another very important property: *the air above the inversion is usually very much drier than the air below it.*

This is caused by the fact that over the height change corresponding to the increase in temperature, the water vapour content (humidity) of the air drops rapidly.

The presence of a subsidence inversion inhibits the vertical movement of the air and so limits the development of cloud. Further, because the air above the inversion is much drier than that below it, the formation of clouds is limited.

Which helps explain why high pressure is usually associated with fine wheather. Any clouds that develop have limited vertical extent and thus the risk of rainfall is low. The cloud type is usually stratocumulus . . .

This applies particularly in summer, but in winter the inversion can trap a layer of cloud and cut out the sun. The layer cloud can even become thick enough to give drizzle or light snow if it is very cold.

Temperature inversions also occur in the atmosphere for other reasons.

For example at night under clear skies the ground cools quickly and as a result the air in the lower levels is also cooled. In conditions of calm or very light winds a layer of cold air several hundred feet thick builds up and a surface inversion occurs.

This situation can be seen in winter in frost hollows, where at the bottom frost is thick but it only extends to a certain height, beyond which the temperature is above freezing.

In this case the conditions are similar to those of a subsidence inversion in that the air in the lower levels tends to have a much higher humidity than that aloft.

For a low pressure system it is usual to find that the temperature decreases with height, although once again in certain meteorological conditions anomalies can occur. For example when there are "Fronts" associated with the low pressure.

A "Front" is the boundary that develops between air masses of differing characteristics and we will now take a look at air masses because correct identification of the air mass likely to prevail is an important part of preparing a forecast.

AIR MASSES (Northern Hemisphere)

Air masses are characterised by their source for example:

Arctic(A); Polar(P); Tropical(T); Equatorial(E)

and also by the track they follow as they move over the Earth's surface. If they spend a lot of time flowing over the sea, then they are said to **"Maritime"(m)**.

On the other hand a long journey over a land mass and they become known as **"Continental"(c)**.

The source characteristics of the Air Masses that affect the UK and Western Europe are as follows:

Arctic Maritime(Am): Initially very cold and dry as it comes off the ice pack, but it soon encounters warm seas . . .

Arctic Continental(Ac): Bitterly cold and very dry . . .

Polar Continental(Pc): In winter it is bitterly cold and extremely dry, in summer it is hot and very dry . . .

Tropical Continental(Tc): In winter it tends to be warm or mild and in summer it produces a heat wave . . .

Tropical Maritime(Tm): All year round it is warm and moist. In winter it gives extensive fog on windward coasts and high ground, often with drizzle. In summer inland and towards the east coast it produces fine warm conditions, as the day progresses . . .

Returning Polar Maritime(rPm): At source it is very cold and dry but a long passage to the south over warmer seas gives it properties that resemble Tropical Maritime, but within the air mass there is latent instability which can give rise to showers or thunder when it flows over hot land in summer.

Equatorial(E): Always very moist and hot, this air mass rarely, if ever reaches our shores . . .

As the air masses move away from their sources so they become modified, especially in the lower levels by the nature of the surface over which they flow.

This results in typical weather characteristics for each air mass by the time they reach the UK.

The cold air masses flowing southwards over a warm sea tend to become "unstable" which means that there is considerable vertical movement of the air.

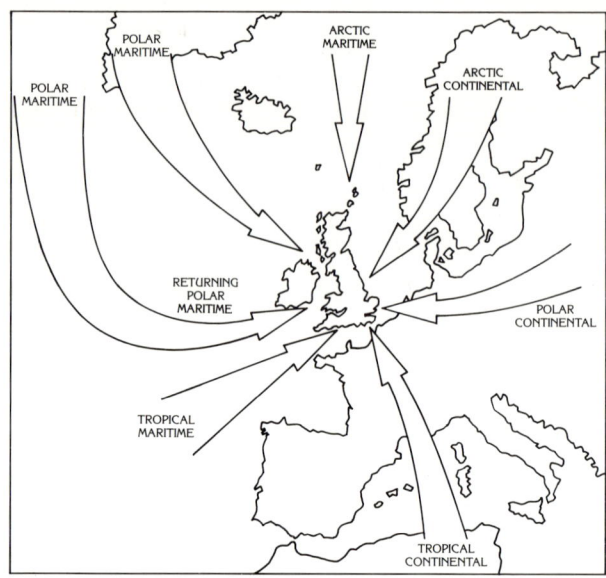

Whereas the warm air masses arriving at our shores from the south tend to be cooled in the lower levels making them 'stable', which means little or no vertical movement of the air and the existence of possible low level inversions.

Weather in Maritime Air Masses

	POLAR (unstable)	TROPICAL (stable)
Surface Wind	Northerly with gusts.	Southwesterly usually steady
Weather	Showers, some heavy snow, possible hail & thunder.	Sea & coast fog; Cloudy/drizzle. Warm inland in summer later in day.
Visibility	Very good outside showers.	Often poor due to coast & hill fog.
Temperature	Cold or very cold in wind.	Mild; can be very warm away from windward coasts.
Humidity	Usually low	High

Pressure	Usually rising; if very quickly then showers die out.	Usually steady with only small changes.
Diurnal change	Showers & gusts die out inland but continue on windward coasts. Frost in sheltered areas as skies clear inland & temperature falls quickly.	Low cloud spreads inland; hill fog becomes extensive; perhaps drizzle. Only small falls in temperature.

Weather in Continental Air Masses

These can be considered under two general headings: Winter and Summer.

In winter the land is much colder than the sea and in summer the reverse is the case.

Surface Wind		At all times it has an easterly component, ranging from NE to SSE. It is often gale force or has strong gusts, in winter.
Weather	**Winter:**	Bitterly cold with snow showers especially along the east coast.
	Summer:	Can give coastal fog in east, but fine inland. A risk of thunder developing if hot & humid.
Visibility	**Winter:**	Good outside snow showers.
	Summer:	Often becomes hazy, poor in sea & coastal fog.
Temperature	**Winter:**	Below freezing, bitterly cold in wind.
	Summer:	Cool near coasts, hot inland.
Humidity	**Winter:**	Very low.
	Summer:	Can be very high.
Pressure	**Winter:**	Often very high and steady.
	Summer:	Usually steady, below 1016mb with slight falls by day.

It frequently occurs that air masses of widely differing characteristics come into close contact due to their circulation around pressure patterns that are semi-permanent features of the Earth's atmosphere.

For example over Canada and Northern USA during the winter the air becomes very cold and dry and there is a tendency for a high pressure system to develop. This is typical over the higher latitudes of all large continental land masses in winter.

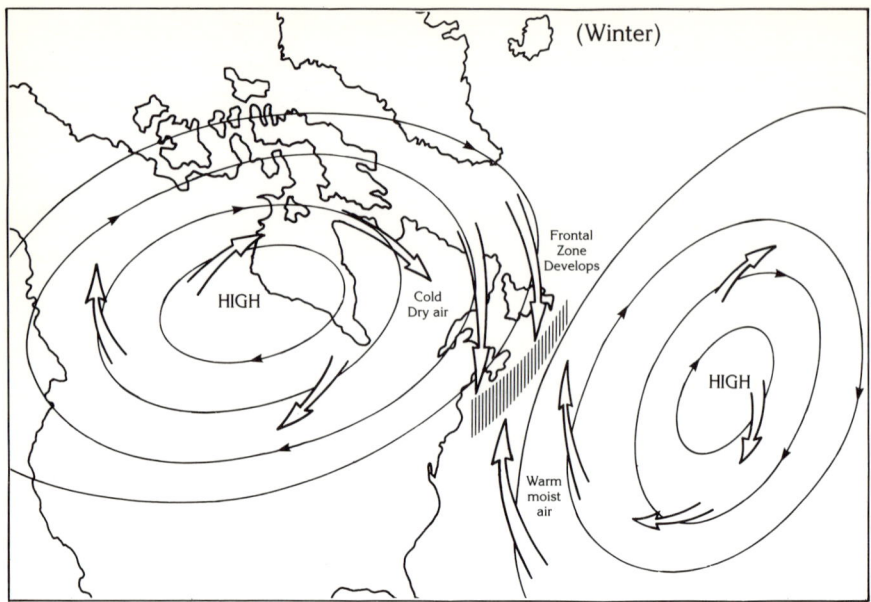

The high over Canada pushes cold dry air eastwards on its northern and eastern sides. The movement of air is subjected to the Coriolis effect causing it to move to the right, with the result that it flows out into the Atlantic . . .

Meanwhile, over the Atlantic ocean in the sub-tropical region the pattern is also one that favours high pressure..the Azores High...which has warm moist air associated with it. The circulation of this high pushes warm moist air westwards on its southern and western flanks. The air in motion is deflected to the right due to Coriolis and flows towards the coast of Canada . . .

The result is that the two air masses are in effect heading towards each other and so the cold dry continental air mass comes into contact with the warm moist Atlantic air, and a "Front" begins to form.

The process is such that the warm moist air rises above the cold dry air because it is less dense. This mass ascent leads to the reduction in surface pressure and the eventual development of low pressure systems, known as "Frontal Depressions" . . .

At the frontal zone the warm air does not rise vertically, instead it "slides up" over the cold air ahead. This has the effect of cooling the warm air (Boyle's Law) which leads to condensation of the water vapour into clouds.

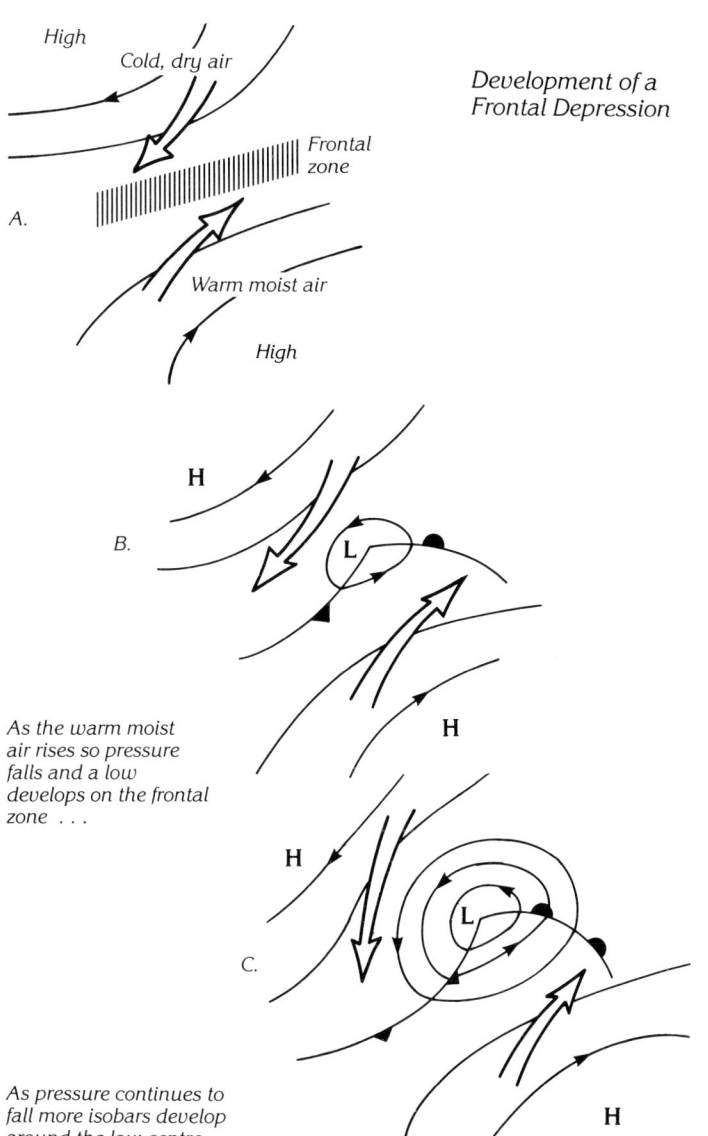

Development of a Frontal Depression

When the pressure at the centre of a low falls it is said to deepen.

As the warm moist air rises so pressure falls and a low develops on the frontal zone . . .

As pressure continues to fall more isobars develop around the low centre . . .

Because the ascent occurs over a large area and extends to great height, some of the clouds are composed of ice crystals, but lower in the atmosphere where the temperature is above freezing they consist of water droplets. Thick layers of cloud build up and eventually precipitation occurs. Depending upon the surface temperature this can be either snow or rain.

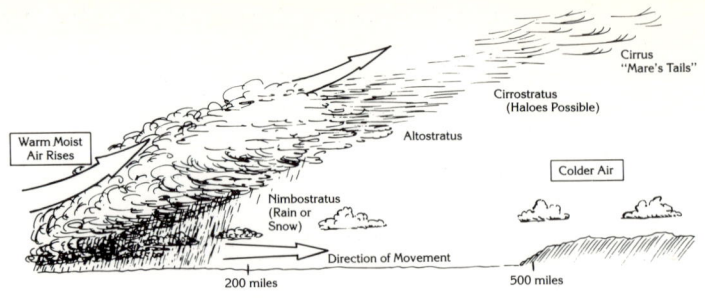

A: *Typical warm front cloud*

A low is also called a depression . . .

As the pressure falls the low develops its own circulation and starts to "suck in" cold air on its western side. Because it is dense it forces the warm moist air ahead of it to rise.

This forced ascent leads to a different build up of cloud compared with the more gentle ascent associated with the warm air.

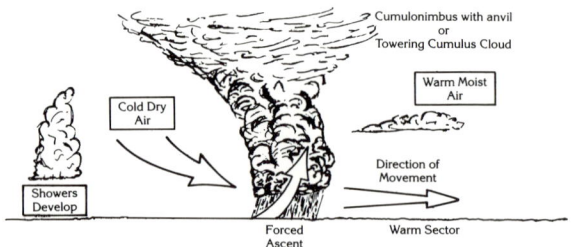

B: *Typical cold front cloud*

Combining A & B gives the classic cross-section through a frontal depression.

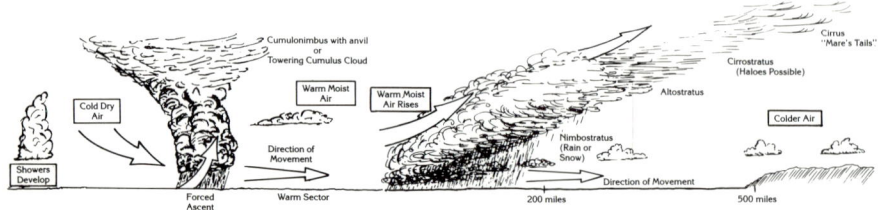

A & B = *Frontal depression cloud structure*

In addition to the patterns associated with depressions and anticyclones at which we have already looked, there are other distributions of pressure that are typical of certain types of weather.

Nowadays, many people are familiar with isobaric charts because they are often shown on TV and in newspapers.

Therefore, it is useful to take a look at some of the typical pressure patterns.

Since isobars are similar to the contour lines used to indicate height on a map, the analogy with the shape of the ground is used in certain cases:

For example a Ridge of high pressure is similar to a headland that separates two bays . . .

A Col is the area of slack pressure that lies between centres of major systems . . .

A Trough of low pressure is similar to a valley . . .

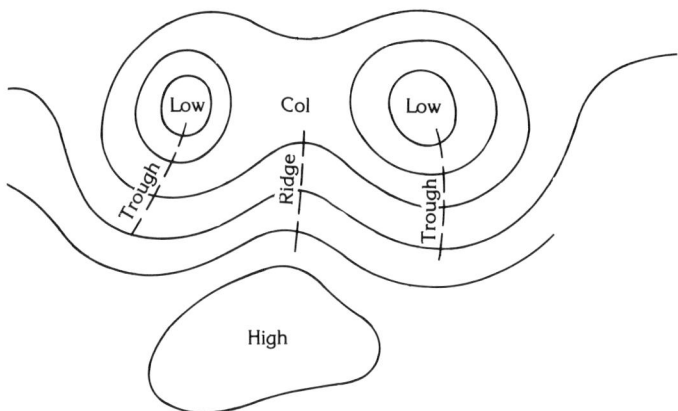

A Warm Front is indicated by a curved line with half circles on it which indicate the direction of movement of the warm air.

A Cold Front consists of a curved line with spikes to indicate the direction of movement.

An Occlusion is indicated by a line with adjacent spike and half circles.

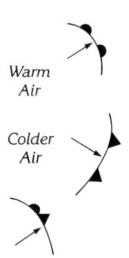

Warm
Air

Colder
Air

An occlusion is the result of the cold air in a frontal depression catching up with the warm air and forcing ascent at the region of contact as shown in the diagram.

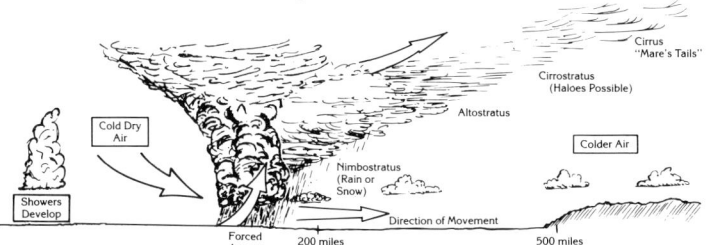

Typical Occlusion Cloud structure

61

Not all areas of low pressure have associated fronts and the following are some examples:

Thermal Lows

Low pressure is associated with air rising, and heating causes the air to rise.

This means that over very hot ground the air starts to rise and an area of low pressure develops, which is known as a thermal low.

Thus over the deserts during the day, especially in summer, pressure tends to be lower than over the sea.

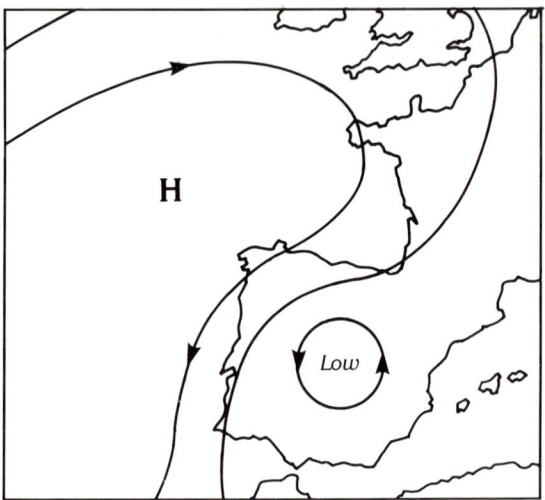

Summer over Iberia . . .

A very good example is over the Iberian peninsula (Spain and Portugal) in the height of summer, when the pressure map almost always indicates a region of low pressure. Some might associate this with bad weather when in fact it is very hot with clear skies and no significant cloud, because the air, even though it is rising and cooling, is so dry that no clouds develop.

This semi permanent thermal low does have an effect off the coast of Portugal because it gives rise to a large change in surface pressure with small change in distance, in other words a steep gradient of pressure. As we have seen this results in strong northerly winds which prevail off the Portuguese coast especially during the afternoons.

Thermal lows of a much smaller scale can develop over the British Isles, more specifically the South and Midlands. In this case the air over the British Isles always contains some water vapour so that clouds can develop. Usually they are large cumulus that build into the classic summer thunderstorms.

In many cases thermal lows tend to disappear at night because nocturnal cooling stops the ascent. However, on a very large scale progressive deepening occurs as in the case of the Monsoon.

A specialised case of a thermal low is known as a Polar Low which can develop in Arctic air streams. As the very cold air moves south over a progressively warmer sea, strong surface heating sets off convection and the cumulonimbus clouds that are formed develop their own circulation.

Polar lows move quickly and are associated with blizzard conditions, and tend to prefer a sea track.

Tornadoes are examples of very localised thermal lows. They are associated with the development of very large cumulonimbus clouds, within which there are violent updrafts and downdrafts of air. In the tornadoes the air is rising at exceptional rate and a very large pressure gradient develops, giving rise to violent winds.

They are similar to the vortex that forms as the water flows down the plug hole of the basin.

Thermal lows of the scale of tornadoes and polar lows are called Instability lows.

Orographic lows owe their existence to the effect of the land upon wind flow. They are to be found in the lee of mountain ranges and disappear as the wind changes direction or decreases in speed.

Often they are indicated by no more than a 'kink' in the isobars.

The patterns of changing pressure are best seen on barograph traces which can be compared with typical weather charts . . .

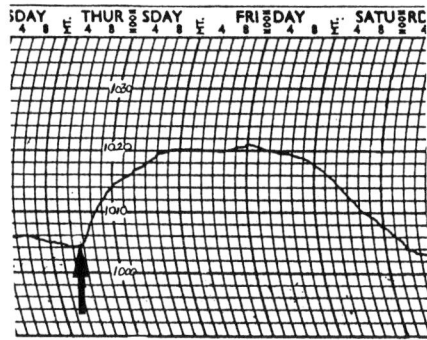

The trace shows the movement of a ridge of high pressure between two mobile frontal depressions.

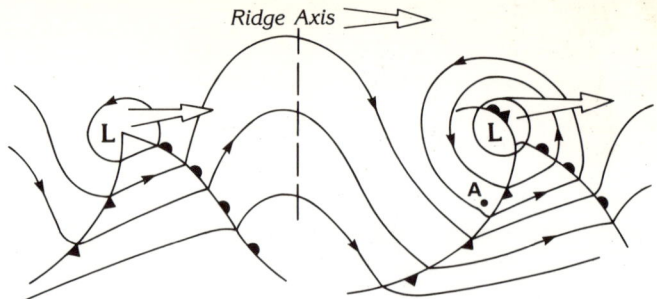

Ridge Axis

The site of the barograph is point A and at Thursday 6 a.m. the pressure map is as shown. At this time the pressure is 1004mb. Throughout the rest of the day the pressure rose steadily to reach 1021mb at noon Friday, which is when the axis of the ridge passed over the site of the barograph.

Thereafter pressure fell steadily as the next depression advanced . . .

This trace reveals a high pressure system which is persisting.

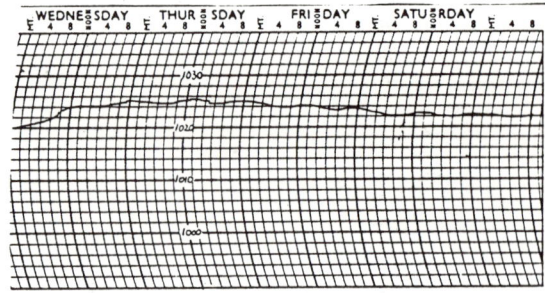

It is interesting because it does show evidence of what is called **"The diurnal variation of pressure".**

Rising pressure in an anticyclone means it is intensifying.

The pressure rises slightly between 4 a.m. and 10 a.m., then falls to a minimum around 4 p.m. rises again until 10 p.m. followed by the fall to 4 a.m. **ALL TIMES ARE LOCAL.**

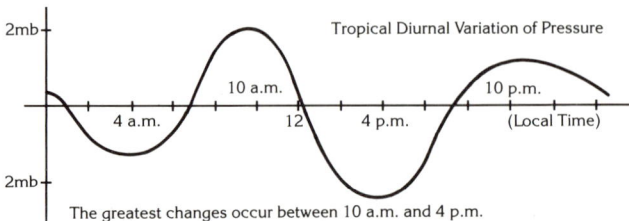

The greatest changes occur between 10 a.m. and 4 p.m.

In the Tropics the range of pressure change is between 2 and 3mb. In the temperate latitudes it is very much smaller and usually masked by other pressure variations.

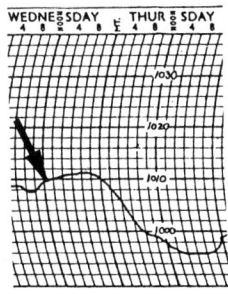

This barograph trace shows the development and movement of a depression. Over the period it deepened in addition to moving quickly eastwards.

At the site of the barograph (point A), Wednesday noon pressure was 1009mb and the corresponding pressure map is shown.

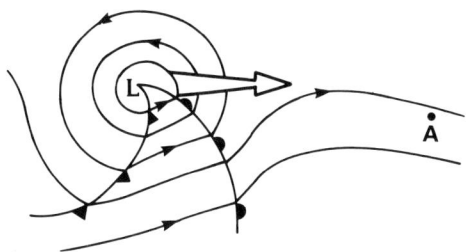

By 10 p.m. (2200) pressure rose to 1011mb, but thereafter it fell rapidly.

This fall was a combination of the movement of the low centre towards the site A and its intensification as the central pressure dropped.

By 4 p.m. (1600) Thursday the centre had passed to the north and over the next 4 hours the cold front cleared the area and pressure began to rise, as the corresponding pressure map shows.

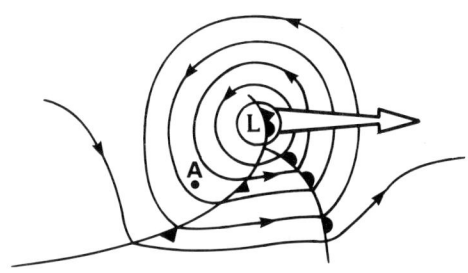

The Altimeter

One of the earliest uses for the barometer was in the measurement of height but it was not until the invention of the aneroid capsule that this principle was developed into a practicable instrument.

The subsequent invention of the aeroplane led to a modification of these barometers so that the dial was calibrated to read height with the result that the "Altimeter" became the standard instrument.

However, in making the graduations in feet it is necessary to assume that the temperature decreases with increase in height at a standard rate. The assumptions are:

a. At the level where the pressure is 1013.2mb the temperature is 15C;

b. Up to about 11km(36,000ft) the temperature lapse rate is 6.5C per kilometre(about 1C per 500ft).

c. Above a height of 36,000ft the temperature is constant at minus 56.5C.

The important point about the altimeter is that it must be set so that it reads zero at mean sea level, but since its action depends upon pressure and the pressure varies over time and from place to place, the setting must be constantly adjusted.

It is usual to use the pressure at the airfield at the time, to adjust the altimeter to read zero height. Thus when the aircraft takes off its height above the airfield is indicated.

This would be fine if all airfields were at the same height above sea level.

But they are not.

Therefore as the aircraft flies from one to another the altimeter must be reset using the local pressure at the time of arrival.

Another very important point for a pilot to understand is how the pressure might vary over his route.

For example if he sets off from an airfield with the local pressure set then his altimeter reads zero on take off.

Suppose that he is flying towards lower pressure. Then if he makes no adjustment for the decrease in pressure his altimeter will always read high. Flying at what he thinks is a constant height he will in fact be getting progressively lower, with obvious dangers . . .

If the pressure is also falling rapidly as he flies towards his destination and he makes no adjustment to his altimeter setting on route, then the situation is extremely hazardous.

This explains why there is a need for constant updating of the surface pressure and why it must be corrected so that barometer readings wherever they are taken are free from sources of possible error.

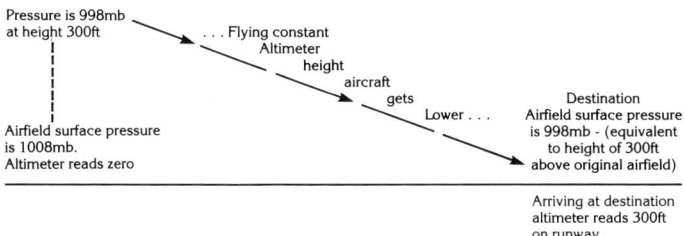

It may be that you have a barometer that has other instruments with it. It is usual to combine a barometer with a thermometer which indicates temperature and a hygrometer that shows humidity, that is the moisture content of the air.

Unlike the barometer which operates perfectly well indoors, these other two tell you little or nothing about the weather outside. Unless they have access to the changing conditions out of doors they will merely tell you what is happening in your home.

Thus the thermometer will give the current room or hallway temperature, and if there is a radiator nearby it is not always representative.

Whilst the hygrometer will record inside humidity. In modern houses this is fairly low and bears no relation to what is really happening in the air mass outside.

So these other two are of limited use . . .

PRESSURE POINTS

Because of the way in which pressure changes with the weather and since it decreases with height, when you think about it, life does have its 'ups and downs' in more sense than one.

Suppose one day the surface pressure is 1030mb, but, because a deep depression has moved in, by the next day it has fallen to 960mb.

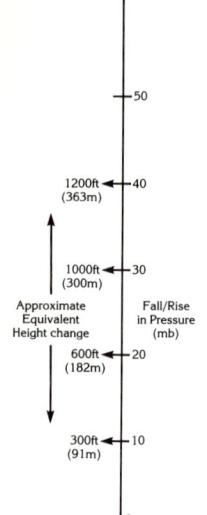

This fall in pressure of 70mb is equivalent to a change in height of about 2200ft!

In other words it is as if we have climbed 2200ft up a mountain . . . no wonder we sometimes feel "under the weather!"

Take the example of pressure falling rapidly at a rate of 6mb every 3 hours. This is an equivalent rise in height of about 60m(180ft) in 180 minutes. In other words, we are effectively rising at lm every 3 minutes (1ft per minute) . . .!

Very rapid decrease in surface pressure due to deep depressions are thought to cause the release of methane gas in some mines with obvious danger of an underground explosion.

This happened on 24 March 1986 when coal pits in the north of England were closed because of a build up of methane as very low pressure passed across the region.

The same low pressure system was thought to be responsible for an explosion in a bungalow in Derbyshire. Built on a landfill site it is thought that the sudden pressure drop associated with the depression resulted in a release of methane from the underground decaying rubbish and this caused the explosion.

The opposite effect is experienced when there is a rapid rise in pressure, which is similar to descending into a mine.

If you recall, compressing a gas raises its temperature and thus, rapid pressure rises can cause problems in deep mine shafts, by giving large temperature rises.

Some significant pressure related events are the following:—

In 1982 the pressure in the outer Hebrides fell to around 930mb (27.5in) . . .

The central pressure of the system responsible for the "Great Storm of October 15/16th 1987" was about 960mb (28.35in).

The problems were caused by the rapidly rising barometer as the storm centre moved quickly away into the North Sea. This created a series of violent gusts that reached speeds of 160kph(100mph) . . . (See p. 38).

OCTOBER 1987
15th   16th

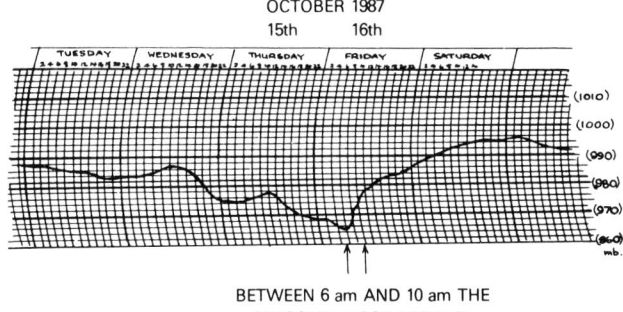

BETWEEN 6 am AND 10 am THE
PRESSURE ROSE RAPIDLY.

The Storm of 25 January 1990 (which is "Burn's day" in Scotland) was a much larger system that moved slowly. The winds associated with it were a result of the large pressure gradient. Lowest central pressure was about 950mb (28.05in). Severe gales covered a much larger area of the British Isles reaching 145kph(90mph) in places . . . (See p. 39).

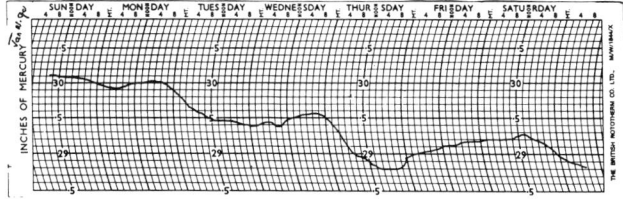

The lowest recorded pressure over the North Atlantic was probably around 915mb(27in) between Greenland and Iceland on 14th December 1986 . . .

The pressure at the centre of Tropical Revolving storms (known as Hurricanes in the West Indies and east Pacific . . . Typhoons in the west Pacific . . . Cyclones in the Indian Ocean, Australia and south Pacific) is always thought of as being very low but often it is not much lower than a good North Atlantic depression.

However the lowest pressure ever recorded was 870mb(25.7in) in the eye of a Typhoon when it was 500km(300m) west of Guam on 12 October 1979 . . .

Tropical storms are also associated with some severe pressure drops. In the Phillipines an average fall of about 27mb per hour!

69

was reported in a typhoon in 1939. This is equivalent to a rise in height of about 4m(13ft) per minute . . .

In 1943 in the Caribbean a fall of 40mb in just 20 minutes occurred, that's equal to a height increase of 363m(1200ft)! . . .

Probably the greatest fall in the British Isles occurred at Stornoway on the Isle of Lewis in the Outer Hebrides When on 20th January 1884 pressure dropped 32.5mb in 4 hours. This is an equivalent height increase of about 300m(1000ft) in 240 minutes, that is 1.25m(4ft) per minute!

Rapid rises are also possible of course and a good example was on October 16 1987 as the low responsible for the Great Storm moved away.

Pressure tendencies of over 23mb in 3 hours were reported over southern England.

The highest was at Royal Naval Air Station Portland where the barometer rose 25.5mb in 3 hours, making it the largest tendency ever reported in the British Isles. That is rising or falling barometers.

The same storm moving away gave a rise of just over 12mb in one hour near Bournemouth.

Elsewhere a rise of l9mb in one hour was recorded in January 1949 in southeast Iceland.

Some truly amazing changes occurred at a weather ship in the centre of the Atlantic on 29 January 1972. The barometer fell 25mb in 90 minutes, it then climbed steeply by 22mb in the next half hour, followed by a further rise of 16mb in subsequent hour!.

That certainly put pressure on the crew! . . .

Pressure can even effect the height of the tide. The predictions for high and low water are calculated assuming an average barometric pressure.

Differences from the average of 34mb(1in) can cause a difference in the height of the tide of about 0.3m(1ft).

Low pressure will tend to raise sea level and a high pressure system will depress it.

This effect, especially with a deep depression and high winds occurring at the time of high spring tide, can lead to flooding.

FORECASTING HINTS

Always try to have a look at a current weather map to get an idea of how the pressure is expected to behave . . .

Remember falling pressure can be caused by movement of a low centre towards you or by the deepening of a centre nearby . . .

If the pressure starts to fall rapidly, that is at a rate greater than 3mb every 3 hours, then expect the wind to BACK and increase giving possible GALES . . .

. . . watch the sky for the increase in upper cloud as perhaps a warm front approaches with the onset of rain...or snow if the air temperature is less than 3C . . .

Rapidly rising pressure suggests that the wind will VEER and strong gusts will develop in addition to strong surface winds . . .

. . . if the air is cold expect heavy showers perhaps with sleet, hail or snow, but with continued rapid rise they should die out . . . overnight ground or air frost is likely if winds die down.

East winds in winter associated with high pressure bring very cold air from the continent with possible snow . . . expect a "black frost" because the air is very dry . . .

. . . watch the weather maps for the development of Low pressure systems over France which help increase the east winds to gale force, giving blizzards . . .

In summer in east winds associated with high pressure you can expect fog to persist along the east coast. This will move inland overnight, before clearing next day.

Sometimes in winter this fog does not clear, giving what is known as "anticyclonic gloom" . . .

Southwest winds from high pressure in summer can give fog along south and west facing coasts, but inland hot sunny weather can be expected . . .

In winter the fog thickens to give drizzle overnight and it moves inland, cloaking the higher ground and often not clearing during the day . . .

Use the wind direction to try to identify the prevailing Air Mass, then refer to the typical weather patterns . . .

Remember, shower clouds rely on surface heating to set them off. At night the ground cools so they tend to die away inland but can continue near windward coasts and over the sea . . .

Very cold air flowing over a warm or hot surface will generate convection which may lead to large clouds and wintry showers, but will always give low level turbulence in the form of gusts . . .

Cold dry air is more likely to give frost than warm moist air . . .

Warm moist air forced to rise by high ground will give fog on the summit . . .

High humidity, hot weather and relatively low pressure are conducive to the formation of thunderstorms which usually break out during the late afternoon or evening . . .

Look for haloes around the sun or moon, they could be the sign that a warm front is approaching...but NEVER look directly at the sun . . .

Convection leading to the build up of cloud requires a specific temperature depending upon the air mass lapse rate. Thus at first light the sky may be clear and this will continue until the sun rises sufficiently to heat the ground and set the air in upward motion. So that by mid-morning large cumuliform clouds are building . . . (See p. 37).

Well, there you have it: a comprehensive look at pressure, the barometer and how you can set about preparing your own forecasts.

Use your barometer, remember it is not just an ornament!